Following Your Path

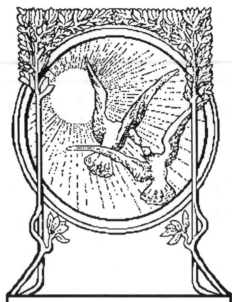

Be at peace with your soul, then heaven and earth will be at peace with you. Enter eagerly into the treasure house that is within you and so you will see the things that are in heaven; for there is but one single entry to them both. The ladder that leads to the kingdom is hidden within your soul. Dive into yourself and your soul will discover the stairs by which to ascend.

Isaac of Nineveh

Following Your Path

A Self-Discovery Adventure Journal
Using Myths, Symbols and Images

By
Alexandra Collins Dickerman

New
DIMENSIONS

P.O. Box 1352, Fair Oaks, California, 95628-1352

Following Your Path
A Self-Discovery Adventure Journal Using Myths, Symbols and Images

Published by:

 DIMENSIONS   P.O.Box 1352, Fair Oaks, CA 95628-1352

Copyright © 1989 by Alexandra Dickerman
Printed in the United States of America

Publisher's cataloguing in Publication Data
Dickerman, Alexandra C.
Following Your Path: A Self-Discovery Adventure Journal Using Myths, Symbols and Images
Psychology, Self-Help, Psychoanalysis
D55 158.1
Library of Congress Catalog Card Number: 89-63485
ISBN 0-99624170-7-6: $19.95 Softcover

Acknowledgements

For permission to use copyright material, the author makes the following acknowledgements:

Harper and Row, to quote from Mircea Eliade's <u>Myths, Dreams and Mysteries.</u>
Princeton, Bollingen, to quote from Joseph Campbell's <u>Hero With a Thousand Faces</u>.
<u>The Gnostic Religion</u> by Hans Jonas, copyright © 1963, by Hans Jonas. Reprinted by permission of Beacon Press.
<u>The Penguin Dictionary of Saints</u> by Donald Attwater (Penguin Classics, 1965), copyright © Donald Attwater, 1965.
<u>The Gospel According to Thomas</u>, by A. Guillaumont, et al. Copyright © 1959 by E.J. Brill. Reprinted by permission of Harper and Row Publishers, Inc.

Grateful acknowledgement is also made for permission to use pictures from the Rider-Waite Tarot Deck, which is reproduced by permission of U.S. Games, Inc., Stamford CT, 06902, Copyright © 1971 by U.S. Games Systems. Further reproduction is prohibited.

Grateful Acknowledgement is also made to Grimaud, Paris, for permission to use pictures from the Greater Trumps of the Marseilles Tarot Deck.

The alchemical illustrations are from old Alchemical texts. Many of these pictures can be found in Jung's <u>Psychology and Alchemy</u>.

If we have infringed upon any copyright material, we offer apologies, and we will give appropriate acknowledgements in all future editions.

I am grateful for the help and support I received from my husband John, and from my daughters, Lexa, and Sarah. I am also grateful to Lori Chaplin, Marian Flanders, Mary Mc Hugh, Doris Dickerman, Tom Dickerman, Tyrell Collins-Conway, and to all the friends and students who took classes and gave me ideas and encouragment.

Dedicated to everyone who travels the path to wholeness.

Table of Contents

Contents

Introduction

In following your path you will face the most important issues in your life and you will learn to grow through them.

Your own path is the way to find yourself, and those things in your life which will bring you satisfaction and fulfillment.

This illustration of Don Quixote by Gustave Dore can serve us as an image of the self, following the path on its quest for fulfillment.

Reaching Your Inner Self

Ordinarily, we are only partially aware of the ideas and feelings going on within ourselves. The other portions lie hidden from us in the realm of the unconscious.

But to live whole, full lives we need to be able to understand and to be in harmony with the inner, as well as the outer world.

We can explore the depths of the psyche by studying our dreams, but they often appear remote and are usually inaccessible for examination without the aid of analysis. But through the use of myths, symbols, and images it is possible to get a glimpse of the secrets from within which silently influence our lives.

The psychoanalyst Carl Jung said that we need to establish the basis for a dialogue with the inner self by using the symbols and images of our unconscious mind that can be recognized and responded to by our conscious mind.

The purpose of this book is to begin the dialogue with our inner mind. Each chapter represents one stage in the journey inward where we can uncover the truths and wisdom of the world within.

As you travel through these pages you will learn the language of the unconscious, allowing your outer and your inner selves to exist in a state of harmony and balance, with each contributing with the other for a full, rich and whole existence.

Remember that this is a workbook. It will have more value to you if you work on the exercises and techniques as you come to them, rather than attempting to read straight through.

If you should come to an exercise which asks for a response that does not come readily to mind, skip it. A forced answer will be self-conscious and it will probably have very little meaning.

Your experience with these materials can be seen as your own adventure into the realms of the powerful unknown. By the time you have completed your journey, you will have established a language of communication with your unconscious self, and you will have a journal of your progress, as well.

❦x❦

How to Use this Book

We are often unaware of the many factors which determine how we feel and how we act because they are hidden from us, deep within the unconscious mind.

In this book, we will explore the realms of the unconscious mind, using myths, symbols and images to identify our hidden motivations and to understand the mysterious inner forces that affect our daily lives. When we understand our true natures, we can learn to utilize our innate wisdom, which can lead us to satisfaction and fulfillment.

The exercises that follow are designed to enable you to recognize the voices from inside so that you can find your way clearly and negotiate successfully through the hazards, and alternate routes along your path.

This is a guidebook to the hidden path, the world within, that deep well of the unconscious where there is, in the words of Carl Jung, "Absolute Knowledge."

Each chapter that follows begins with a Tarot Card. Each card contains powerful symbols representing one step along your journey to self-discovery. There are also pictures, exercises, stories, fables and myths which will speak to your psyche in non-literal ways.

As you read each chapter and fill out your responses to the exercises, you will be participating symbolically in the mythic hero's journey, and discovering the basis for many of your own thoughts and feelings.

Use your impulses and hunches to interpret the exercises. You might be asked, for example, to respond to the image of a sword. This exercise might ask you how you feel about the sword, and what it is made of. You will then find a definition for the symbolism of the sword. Comparing your responses to the symbol's definition will enable you to discover a window through which you can peer at the mysterious and powerful world within.

The following example demonstrates how the exercises work:

The **sword** represents power.

The exercise asks you:	The significance of your answer:
How do you feel about it?	This shows how you feel about power. If you like the sword, chances are you like power. If you are afraid of the sword, the indications are that you have a fear of power.
What is the sword made of?	If your sword is made of gold, you undoubtedly prize power. If the sword is made of plastic, ask yourself how you feel about plastic, it will give you an indication of how you feel about power.

You may think you do not understand a chapter, a symbol, or an exercise in any analytical or literal way. Trust your senses and your feelings about what an image means to you, and let your perception gradually evolve. This is the way your unconscious communicates with you when you allow it.

This book is a workbook and a journal; it takes time to go through it. Most people find that they can only spend about a half hour a day on it. And remember, not all parts of the book will make logical sense to you. Much of this material is only intended to be understood intuitively.

Your unconscious is at best an elusive companion. You will be able to find out amazing and important things about yourself when you go through this book The best way to do this is to quiet all outer thoughts and distractions, and to focus your attention inward.

Begin with a relaxation exercise. You may already have your favorite relaxation technique, or you could try the following:

Close your eyes. Quiet your thoughts, and picture a clear blue sky. In the sky you can see a glorious golden sun, which warms and soothes you as you relax all your muscles, and let go of all the tension throughout your body. Your mind is quiet and your body is at peace as you breathe in healing calm, and you breathe out all the stresses and strains from your entire being, and allow yourself to completely, deeply relax.

Before you fill in the sentences for the exercises that follow, take a minute to relax your conscious mind, to allow the responses from your unconscious to emerge. Use the relaxation suggestion above, or simply close your eyes and quiet your mind of all distractions and extraneous thoughts, for at least a minute or two.

After the explanation of the symbolism for each chapter, there is an affirmation, or a short positive message. If you find that you experienced an adverse reaction to an exercise (and there are some loaded symbols, including the Devil and Death), or if any unpleasant feelings have been triggered, repeat the affirmation to yourself as often as necessary until you feel ready to examine the source of your discomfort.

The chapters and the exercises you react to most strongly are those of the most value to you. If you come across a personal demon, you will know that you have reached an opportunity for growth and self-discovery.

Each chapter will provide you with pieces of information and glimpses of insight about yourself and how you feel and why you react to certain things the way you do. Some chapters will be easy and fun; some will seem trivial. And there will be some chapters that will be of immediate, critical importance for you concerning the things you face in your life today.

The order of the chapters follows the progression of your journey. Follow the sequence of the book the first time you go through it. You will no doubt find that you spend most of your time working on the chapters that evoke the most vivid emotional responses.

You may want to embark on this journey again at a later time when your life has changed. When different issues are prevailing, different chapters and exercises will take on new significance, and the symbols will speak to you in new ways.

Bon voyage. Take your time, and enjoy your journey!

The Eight Steps

Scholars of mythology have defined the eight basic steps which comprise the mythic journey. These steps correspond to the symbols on the pictures of the Greater Trumps of the Tarot Cards, which, along with other symbols and pictorial and allegorical imagery, will form the landmarks of the journey which follows.

These are the basic steps of the mythic journey which is undertaken by the hero, or the psyche:

Step I. Birth

Step II. Initiation

Step III. Withdrawal

Step IV. Quest

Step V. Into the Realms of Death

Step VI. Confrontation with the Devil

Step VII. Rebirth

Step VIII. Transformation

Throughout this book I have used male and female pronouns according to the pictures on the Tarot Cards because a male picture, such as the Emperor, represents your own inner male side, or, in Jungian terms, animus. The female pictures, for example the Empress, represent an aspect of your own inner female side, or anima. In many cases, as with the Fool, where there is no particular gender, the gender is your own. I have used the pronouns matching the pictures to make it simple.

Journey Schedule

As you go through this book, it will help if you have a schedule to keep track of where you are and to help you stay focused. Each chapter could take a day, a week, or even a month, depending on how much time you can put into it and how it affects you.

Date Begun	Finished	
		Step I — Birth
		Chapter 1 — The Fool
		Chapter 2 — The Magician
		Step II — Initiation
		Chapter 3 — The High Priestess
		Chapter 4 — The Empress
		Chapter 5 — The Emperor
		Chapter 6 — The Hierophant
		Step III — Withdrawal
		Chapter 7 — The Lovers
		Chapter 8 — The Chariot
		Chapter 9 — Strength
		Chapter 10 — The Hermit
		Step IV — Quest
		Chapter 11 — The Wheel of Fortune
		Chapter 12 — Justice

Date

Begun Finished

		Step 5 — Into the Realms of Death
		Chapter 13 — The Hanged Man
		Chapter 14 — Death: Change
		Chapter 15 — Temperance
		Step 6 — Confrontation with the Devil
		Chapter 16 — The Devil
		Chapter 17 — The Tower
		Step 7 — Rebirth
		Chapter 18 — The Star
		Chapter 19 — The Moon
		Chapter 20 — The Sun
		Step 8 — Transformation
		Chapter 21 — Judgement
		Chapter 22 — The World

Step I- Birth

You have come to the start of a new cycle. This is your beginning; this is the time of your birth.

Chapter 1
The Fool

The Fool

e begin as the Fool, as we walk off the precipice, in an act of faith which transcends space and time and all known boundaries. The Fool is unformed, encompassing all possibilities, the absolute and the source of all.

THE FOOL.

If a man would persist in his folly, he would become wise.

William Blake

The Fool is a carefree traveler stepping out into the unknown on a quest for wisdom.

To begin your own adventure, you should be feeling relaxed and comfortable. Look at the picture of the Fool on the previous page for several minutes. Notice the details. Close your eyes, and see the picture in your mind. Let your mind wander and let your body relax, as you open your eyes and continue to gaze at the picture. Now allow the picture to appear in your mind. Concentrate on it for a few minutes before you open your eyes.

Once you feel that you are familiar with the picture, finish the sentences on page 6 that follow as spontaneously as you can. Try not to be logical and self-editing, just let the answers flow as they come to you, accepting them without question; there is no right and wrong.

It has been said that images which come from the psyche refer to the psyche. When you allow your responses to the following exercises to come spontaneously and impulsively from your unconscious, you will be able to view hidden parts of yourself.

It is possible to live the fullest life only when we are in harmony with...symbols; wisdom is a return to them. It is a question neither of belief nor knowledge, but of the agreement of our thinking with the primordial images of the unconscious.

Carl Jung

$$\boxed{The\ Fool}$$

magine that you are walking along your path. The day is bright and you feel cheerful, with a sense of openness to the unexpected.

The way is winding and you stop to enjoy the view of the mountains below as you make your way up the narrow path.

Around a turn you arrive at a plateau, where the grass is green and the wild flowers are in bloom.

The sky is clear and the bright sun warms your back in the chill mountain air.

As you walk across the meadow, you see a man, with a dog at his heels. The man, who seems to be wandering aimlessly, is dressed in a brightly colored, slightly garish shirt, with a pack slung over his shoulder. There is a picture of an eagle sewn on the back of his pack. Although he seems to be precariously near the edge of the precipice, he looks cheerfully unconcerned about where he is going.

It looks as if, at any moment, he may just walk off the edge of the cliff, and yet he seems to be completely confident.

As you approach The Fool, you notice that he is holding a white rose in his left hand…

Use your imagination and write down the first answer that comes to mind, completing the following sentences:

The sun shines behind the Fool, giving him _____ on his journey.

He carries a stick over his shoulder. It is his _____

The Fool is carrying a backpack, with the picture of an eagle on it. Inside the pack is _____

for _____

The dog at his heels is his _____

He is stepping out into the unknown, taking all he will need. His heart is filled with _____

The Fool says,
I am _____

I will _____

I can _____

I fear _____

I have _____

The Fool represents you as you embark on a new stage of your life. This figure stands for adventure and openness to new experiences.

The sun reresents the all-seeing divine force, the center of intuitive understanding.

The stick is like a wand, it represents magical powers the Fool will posess on his journey.

The backpack the Fool carries is a place where things that are valued or precious are kept.

The picture of an eagle symbolizes release from bondage, strength and victory.

The dog represents companionship, fidelity and watchfulness.

What do your responses to the exercise of the Fool tell you about your feelings as you begin this adventure? How did you feel about the sun, or divine, intuitive energy? See if you can find a relationship between your response to the image, and its definition.

Can you discover anything about your own magical resources from your response to the Fool's stick? What about the pack with the picture of an eagle... can you find out something about your priorities and values by what you have in the pack?

Was the dog, or faithful companion, a positive image...do you have good feelings about companions?

Think about your answers and what they mean about you. Remember, any answer that comes from you uniquely reflects yourself. There is no limit to the variety of choices a person could make in filling out the questions in these exercises. Your answers are particularly your own and they express something important for you to know about yourself.

(Remember that you don't have to have a clear and logical understanding of all your answers. This is not the realm of logic; you will find out as much about yourself from the way you feel about an exercise as from what you think it means.)

Affirmation

Say to yourself:
There are unlimited possibilities and opportunities before me. I know I am protected, accepted, and secure, as I venture out into the unknown.

Looking at...

The White Rose

 magine that you are sitting by a gentle stream on a clear day. The sun is shining brightly. You have a pure white rose in your hand. When this image comes to your mind's eye, complete the following sentences:

The white rose is very _____

I will put this rose _____

I feel _____

about the rose, because _____

This white rose reminds me of _____

The sun is _____

and it makes me feel _____

It gives me this message

_____

Definition

The white rose represents purity, virtue and spirituality, so the way you feel about the white rose is the way you feel about your own spirituality. The answers you gave regarding the sun indicate your feelings about illumination and perfection. See if you can find a link between what you know about yourself and your responses. How do your answers reflect the way you feel? See if you can find a significance to your responses in terms of your life right now.

Your answers today may be different from your answers tomorrow, depending on your frame of mind. Sometimes your answers will be obvious and sometimes they may not seem to make sense until you have thought about them for awhile, but they will always provide you with interesting and important information, and often some surprises.

Starting Off

As we begin our journey, we will soon discover that, in the words of Mircea Eliade, "A change of perspective can have the effect of a profound regeneration of our intimate being." Seeing something familiar in the unfamiliar form of a myth or a symbol can make it become suddenly meaningful. To illustrate this idea, he quotes an old Jewish story about Rabbi Eisik of Cracow. [1]

> The poor, pious Rabbi Eisik, son of Jekel, had a dream in which he was told to travel to Prague where, under the great bridge leading to the royal castle he would find a hidden treasure. The dream was repeated three times, so the old rabbi decided to go to Prague. When he arrived, he found the bridge, but it was guarded day and night so Eisik did not dare to dig.
>
> Finally the captain of the guard, who had seen him loitering and heard his story, asked about the dreams and the guard laughed heartily to hear how the poor rabbi had worn out his shoes coming all the way to Prague just because of his dreams. He said to the rabbi that he, too, had had a dream, in which a voice had told him to go to Cracow to look for a great treasure in the house of a rabbi by the name of Eisik, son of Jekel. The treasure was to be found in a dusty corner buried behind the old stove. But the officer said he was an intelligent man, too rational to put his trust in dreams. The rabbi, with a deep bow thanked the guard and rushed back home, where he dug behind the old stove and found a great treasure, which put an end to his poverty.

"Thus," Eliade quotes Heinrick Zimmer, "the real treasure, that which can put an end to our poverty and all out trials, is never very far. There is no need to seek it in a distant country. It lies buried in the most intimate part of our own house (ourselves) if only we knew how to unearth it.

"And yet, there is this strange and persistent fact that it is only after a pious journey to a distant region, a new land [such as the land of dreams, myths or symbols] that the meaning of that inner voice guiding us on our search can make itself understood by us. And to this strange and persistent fact is added another, that he who reveals to us the meaning of our mysterious inward pilgrimage must himself be a stranger, of another belief and another race." [2]

Our "pious journey to a distant region, a new land" begins with The Fool, who is a stranger.

God is a circle, the center of which
is everywhere and the circumference of which is nowhere.

Hermes Trismegistus

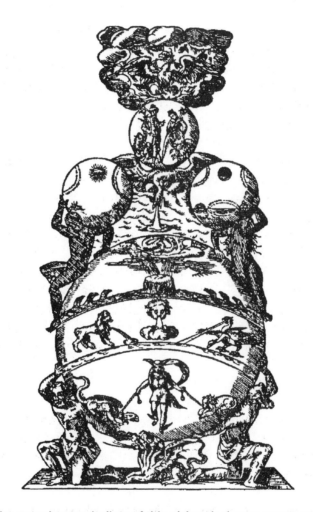

The complex symbolism of this alchemical vase represents
the journey of the Fool, who travels from the lower levels
of material existence to the divinity of the soul.

Chapter 2
The Magician

The Magician represents the subconscious mind in its humanized form. He symbolizes the ability to harness the energies of nature by transcending the ego.

THE MAGICIAN.

The Magician

s you proceed along your path, you come to a thicket. There are dense overhanging vines and you notice a square wooden table standing under a tree.

There are several curious objects on the table. You can see a chalice, a sword, a wand and a coin.

A man is standing in front of the table. He seems to be preoccupied, focusing all his attention on what he is doing. In his right hand is a small staff and he is pointing his left hand toward the earth.

Sit comfortably, with no distractions, letting your mind and your body relax. Let go of all tensions before you begin this exercise.

The Magician sits before the table which holds the symbols of the elements of life: earth, air, fire and water.

Red roses grow beside the Magician because _____

White lilies are for_____

The Magician says:

I can _____

I will _____

I am _____

I have _____

I always _____

Now the Magician turns to you with his wand and says:
_____

My message to you is that _____

Definition

The red rose represents earthly passion and fertility.

The lily is considered the counterpart of the lotus in the East. It represents purity, beauty and feminine perfection.

What can you tell about your feelings with regard to passion, purity and the feminine impulse from your answers? (For instance, if you felt that the roses grew because of the Magician's suffering, you may feel that passion engenders suffering.)

The Magician stands for the resources you possess that go beyond your usual physical capabilities. You can find out about the nature of these special faculties from the message the Magician had for you. This is a message about your own magical, or spiritual gifts.

Affirmation

After you have finished the exercise of the Magician, sit quietly and say to yourself:
I have a clear understanding of who I am. I am grounded and in control of myself and my life.

Now, think about yourself and who you are. And think about what you want.

Close your eyes and find your own center.
Connect your center to the earth's center.

Looking at…

The Elements

*magine that you see an old table hidden among thick vines.*

On the table are several objects. You see an old coin.

Where did it come from? _____

How do you feel about it? _____

Next to the coin you see a wand. Where did it come from? _____

How do you feel about it? _____

There is also an old sword. Where did it come from? _____

How do you feel about it? _____

You also see a chalice. Where did it come from? _____

How do you feel about it? _____

Definition

The coin represents the earth, it is the foundation and material life.

The wand represents the air. It is the first element, magical power and freedom.

The sword is fire, which stands for power.

The chalice is water, the source of life.

See if you can find a relationship between the symbol and your response to it. Was one object more compelling than the others? Did you have negative feelings about any of the elements? Did you have any very positive reactions? Think about what you might be able to learn about yourself from your responses.

Guardian of the Spirit

*The Magician goes past the boundaries of the earth
seeking to transcend human nature.*

he Magician possesses the gifts and the powers of the spirit. His capabilities transcend ordinary human nature and the vulnerabilities of the ego. He lives in a world of miracles beyond all logic. He raises one hand toward heaven where he derives his power. He raises his other hand to the earth, where he will use this power. Thus the magician connects the world of the spirit with the world of nature.

The Magician represents the subconscious mind in its humanized form. He represents the spiritual quest through which he is able to vanquish the internal primitive forces of darkness.

For example, the seven deadly sins (the sins of anger, avarice, envy, gluttony, pride, lust and sloth), are forces which can chain us to the ego, to the earth, and to the material world.

The Magician is capable of producing a miracle, or an event which goes past logic and overcomes the natural limitations of life:

> *Buddha tells us that the magician, "Enjoys marvelous power in its several different modalities: from being one, he becomes several; having become several, he again becomes one; he becomes visible or invisible, he passes, without feeling any resistance, through a wall, a high rampart or a hill as if it were air: he dives from on high down through the solid earth as though water; he walks upon water without sinking in it, as though on firm land..."* [3]

In different cultures around the world, the shaman or the medicine man possesses various amazing powers, such as being able to walk on hot coals and to endure extreme cold. These abilities transcend what we believe to be ordinary human capabilities and yet they are performed by humans who have been trained in mystical traditions.

What meaning can the powers of the Magician have for us? Let us look, with open minds, into the mysterious depths of life which we have long neglected in over-enthusiasm for the material world.

The Magician is capable of producing a miracle, or an event which overcomes the natural limitations of life.

Using Mythology to Discover the Magical Powers of the World Within

The place of myths and the imagination, the qualities of the inner life, which can guide us to different kinds of illumination, cannot be proved by observable fact. These are the means through which we can experience personal transformations, which can only occur within ourselves.

Myth is the secret opening through which the inexhaustible energies of the cosmos pour into human cultural manifestation. Religion, philosophies, the arts, the social forms of primitive and historic man, prime discoveries in science and technology, the very dreams that blister sleep, boil up from the basic, magic ring of myth.

Joseph Campbell 4

The images of mythology are common to all mankind. According to Carl Jung, they are instinctive; they come from within us, regardless of what our environment or experiences have been.

Myths are composed of universal archetypes, or universal models. These archetypes are the same everywhere in the world. In different cultures, there are different details, depending upon the local geographic, climatic, racial and other features, but the essential forms and ideas are the same.

Carl Jung investigated and interpreted these universal archetypes in his study of psychology, calling them the "Archetypes of the Collective Unconscious." He found that all people use the same images to depict the same experiences and feelings.

The object of mythology is to explain the world, to make experience intelligible and give it meaning. Myth serves as a mirror for our inner life. This is the function and meaning of the mythologies of the world. They reflect the inner experiences of the people who created them.

We can use myths to examine and attempt to understand our own lives; we can gaze into the mirror of mythology to find our own inner reflections.

The theme of redemption through love can be seen in the story of the frog prince.

Throughout this book, myths, fairy tales, and folklore are used to illuminate a particular aspect of human life on a psychological level. Myths (and their domestic counterparts, fairytales and folklore) will reveal to our consciousness the activity of the inner self, or the psyche.

When you read these myths and fairy tales, try to understand them in terms of your own emotional experiences. You may, for example, see yourself as Isis, (see chapter 3) trying to put all the fragments and bits of experience and information together to recreate something, (Osiris), or to develop an idea or to complete a project, as in the myth, when Isis bore the child Horus.

By looking at ourselves and our lives through the mirror of mythology, we can see things which we are otherwise too close and too attached to recognize. We can evaluate our situations and their context from a detached, almost impersonal point of view when we meet them in the form of a fable or a fairy tale. In this way we may gain a perspective which will give us new insights and answers to real-life questions.

The mirror was used as a symbol of truth-seeking in Snow White.

As you come upon a myth or fable, read it and then pause to consider how it might serve as a metaphor to explain a situation or a condition of your own life. Examine the myth. What were the obstacles facing the protagonist? Who was the antagonist? How was the task or situation finally resolved? What contribution was the hero able to make after returning from the adventure? Look at the myth for the secrets it may reveal to you about your own situation. What obstacles do you face? Who or what is your enemy? What is the solution? What can you gain, and give to others as a result of your experience?

The images of myths are shadows from the depths. Myths can direct our minds and hearts to the mysteries of all existence. Contained within each myth or fairy tale is a metaphor for the experiences in life we all have. Myths can guide us when we become lost or disoriented; they can be used to help us understand ourselves and to define which parts of ourselves are in conflict.

There is an example of a technique similar to this use of myths for self enlightenment from Dahomey, Africa, where a person who has a problem visits a sorcerer who will "draw the Fa", or throw date pits to determine which of their gods is prevailing in his situation. Each god is associated with a corresponding myth, which the enquirer examines for its relevance in his own problem. Because each god has a myth which indicates a type of response, by being directed to a god, the seeker is given a suggestion of guidance. In this way the person is freed of uncertainty and able to make up his mind about how to proceed. [5]

o understand a myth and to relate to it meaningfully is to rediscover the unknown- the magic in life. You can do this by searching for the intrinsic meaning a myth has for you. You can begin this process by recognizing that the hero's journey is really the journey of your own psyche.

There is a universal pattern or form which all myths seem to follow, with infinite variations according to the time, place, and teller of the myth. In general, myths tell of the path of the hero, who is ourself. The hero goes through an experience of separation from the world, to an experience of initiation, in which he or she assimilates powers at their source, and then he returns home. The hero goes off from the ordinary, everyday world into a region of the supernatural, where strange forces are found. After an encounter with his adversary, the hero wins a decisive victory and then returns to the world with the power to bestow the benefits of his adventure on the world.

The path this book will take leading us on the journey inward is the same path a hero in a myth or folktale follows.

The hero, then, leaves the point of origin to embark on an adventure of the soul. The adventure begins with a battle, abduction, dismemberment, or crucifixion, or the hero might go off into the night sea or into the belly of a whale. At this point, the psyche is fragmented and he feels lost and confused. After various tests, and often with the aid of some magical helpers, the hero returns, victorious. He completes his task and unlocks a secret, finds a missing object or participates in a sacred marriage. The hero escapes the underworld or magical forest or enchanted castle and returns to be resurrected or rescued and to bring light from the darkness into the world. In a fairy tale, the triumphs of the hero are domestic. In a myth, the whole society is regenerated and it is the history of the world that is affected.

The hero goes off on the adventure of the soul.

This parallels the nature of all life, the cycle of history and of individual maturity. All things and beings in the world come from an original source. They grow and experience the expression of their power and then flow back into the original state from which they came. In scientific terms, this is the law of conservation of energy. In religious terms, it is the law of God. It is the law of the cosmos and the nature of existence.

The hero is always to be found within ourselves. The adventures of the hero are those of our own psyche as it ventures into the depths to do battle with the subterranean forces and then comes back renewed and victorious.

We experience this adventure on a more mundane level, every day, beginning with the waking state, where all reality is factual. Then in a meditative state or in dreams the essence of reality changes and experience takes on new meanings. This is the level of the unconsciousness where new answers can be found and new ideas born. Then, once again, the psyche returns to the wide-awake, worldly state. This is the adventure each of us takes every night as we drift off into sleep, and dream, to work out the issues of the psyche, where it is said that God is to be found, until we awaken once again, perhaps to bring our renewed understandings and insights out into the light.

This alchemist picture of the hero's armor shows the symbols of his journey.

Step I in Review

In Step I you, the hero, encountered the Fool and the Magician. Their purpose was to help you evaluate your feelings and assess your situation as you embark upon a new cycle in your life.

Write down a brief summary of what you experienced at this beginning point of your quest.

Write down the most important feelings and insights you have gained from your travels through the birth, the first stage of your journey.

Step II- Initiation

Now is the time of your initiation.
You will soon meet four sages, who will
offer you the benefits of their wisdom.

Chapter 3
The High
Priestess

The High Priestess

he High Priestess is the daughter of the moon. She sits between the black and the white pillars of the active and the passive principles, the masculine and the feminine states. She holds the book of the divine law in her lap.

THE HIGH PRIESTESS

Looking at...

The High Priestess

ou have come to the temple of the High Priestess. She sits in a wooded grove holding a book in her lap. She sits between a black and a white pillar.

You must lift the veil and pass between the two pillars.

The air is cool and beyond the grove the wind gently blows through a field of tall corn.

Inside, you see the High Priestess, who seems to stare deep into your very soul as you enter her temple. She appears to be both ancient and timeless.

She greets you and at once you feel that you and she have known one another for a very long time.

She tells you that your tasks will be to learn to distinguish the real from the false, to hear the sound that is silent, and to see the invisible.

The High Priestess says to you "Within yourself is the key and therein all mysteries will unfold."

The High Priestess says:

I am _____

I can _____

I remember _____

I know _____

I will _____

She will give you the knowledge of _____

She will remind you that _____

Definition

The symbol of the High Priestess represents the subconscious mind in its pure state. It is yin–the yielding, gentle, receptive, tolerant, merciful and withdrawn state of mind.

Your responses to the exercise of the High Priestess will provide you with knowledge from within yourself.

The subconscious mind can take scattered fragments of ideas and form them into new ideas ready to be reborn as insights and inspirations.

The High Priestess represents the
subconscious mind in its pure state.

Affirmation

Say to yourself:
All knowledge and understanding are within my reach when I
look within myself.

The Message

The High Priestess has a message for you. She has read your life in the book she holds, and she can read your soul in your eyes.

She wants you to know that _____

She has a gift for you. It is _____

Definition

This is a message to you from your subconscious mind and an indication of the nature of your own innate gifts.

How do you feel about these gifts?

Looking at...

The Two Pillars

The High Priestess suggests that you look more closely at the two pillars at the entrance to her grove. One pillar is black and the other is white.

There is a message for you on the black pillar. It says_____

_____

There is a message on the white pillar. It says _____

_____

You walk between the two pillars. You feel_____

When you have passed through the pillars, you find_____

Definition

The two pillars represent the dual aspect of life. The black pillar is the feminine and the unconscious side; the white pillar represents the masculine, material world. Walking between the pillars represents entering into the world of the psyche.

This exercise will give you some insights about your feelings concerning these two sides of yourself. It will tell how you feel about entering into a new level of self-awareness. What you find on the other side of the pillars is a metaphor for what you will find in your subconscious.

Looking at...

The Scroll

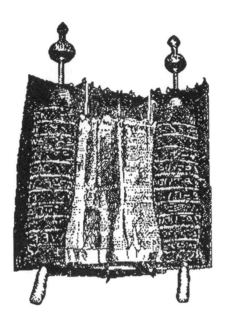

Imagine that you have come upon an ancient scroll.

On it there is a message for you.

It says _____

Definition

> The scroll represents the Book of Life. This exercise will give you some idea of what your own book of life holds at this point along your journey.

The symbol of the High Priestess can be described in terms of the following myth of Isis and Osiris.

The Myth of Isis and Osiris

 hen Osiris came to the throne as Pharoah of Egypt, the Egyptians were very warlike. This was soon altered when he and the Queen, his sister Isis, came into power.

After they had taught the people of the land from the Delta and upper Egypt as far as Thebes the arts of peace and civilization, Osiris left his brother, Set, to rule, and he went off to civilize the people of more distant lands.

When he left, Osiris took no army. He took only a band of priests and musicians. Wherever he went, most of the barbarians of even the wildest tribes were won over by his wise words and sweet music.

But not all the people followed Osiris. There was evil awake in the world, and strife against good. The leader of evil was Set, the younger brother of Isis and Osiris.

As soon as Osiris returned home, Set prepared him a feast of honor. Osiris, suspecting nothing, came unattended. After the meal, Set had a beautiful cedarwood chest inlaid with precious jewels taken into the banquet hall. Then Set said, "Here is my gift to one of the guests. It shall belong to whomever it fits."

All the guests tried to fit into the chest, but it was too tall or too short, too fat or too thin for them. Then Osiris climbed into the chest and it fit him perfectly. Osiris cried out, "The chest is mine! It fits as if it were made for me!"

Isis, Egyptian mother goddess.

"It is indeed yours," cried Set. "It is the chest in which you shall die." He slammed down the lid and had it nailed shut, and sealed it with molten lead. Then he threw it into the Nile.

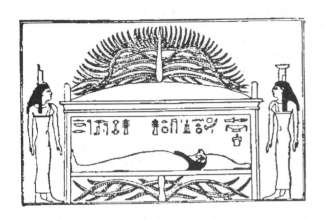

Osiris was shut up in the chest by his brother.

As the chest floated in the sea, a great wave hurled it into a Tamarisk tree. The tree quickly clasped its branches around the chest until it was completely hidden within its trunk.

After many years of searching, Isis finally found the tree which housed the chest. The rulers of that land, Queen Astarte and King Malcander, agreed to give Isis a favor in return for her blessings, and Isis asked them for the Tamarisk tree.

When it was given to her, Isis set the coffin on a boat and sailed off. Finally she reached an island where she hid the chest in the reeds of the Delta until she could perform the funeral rites.

But Set discovered the chest. Enraged, he snatched out the body of his murdered brother and tore it into seven pieces, which he scattered throughout the land of Egypt.

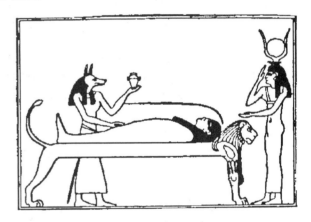

Isis and Anubis (who took the shape of a wild dog) found the pieces to put Osiris together again.

"Now I have destroyed Osiris and kept his spirit out of the afterworld," he cried.

When he was gone, Isis crept out of her hiding place and set out in search of the pieces of her husband's body. Her distress was so great as she rode up and down the Nile, that even the crocodiles pitied her and let her pass.

Isis was able to find all but one piece of the body, with the aid of Anubis, the son of Set and Nepthys, who took the shape of a wild dog to help the search.

Once the pieces of the body were found, Isis performed a magic ritual which put Osiris back together.

Later she and Osiris had a son, whom they named Horus.

When Osiris finally died, his spirit passed into the Duat, where he became King of the Dead, welcoming all those who were found worthy to enter his kingdom and adding them to his army of the blessed with whom he would return to reign on earth after the last great battle with Set.

Once the pieces of Osiris were found, Isis performed a magic ritual which reconstructed and reanimated him.

Osiris represents our immortal, divine side which cannot be destroyed or vanquished; it can come up out of the coffin of molten lead and survive fragmentation and mutilation.

Consider your own life in terms of the symbolism of this myth. Are you collecting fragments of new ideas and information to put them together in the form of a new idea? Or are the parts of yourself and your life so fragmented and scattered that nothing adds up and makes sense? The myth of Isis tells us we can always go back and collect the pieces and put them together to create something new and wonderful.

Looking at...

The Box

Imagine you are inside a box. What does the box look like?

_____

What is it made of?_____

What color is it?_____

Describe the box _____

How do you feel about being inside this box?_____

Can you get out? How?_____

Do you want to get out? _____

Will you get out? When? Why?_____

Definition

The box is the symbol of the material body (containing the unconscious). It will often give you a quick sketch of your present frame of mind.

How did you feel in the box? What does this indicate about the way you are feeling about your life?

What is your box made of? Is it threatening to you or is it comfortable? (Look up the symbolism for the color of your box in the color index.)

Did you feel confined in your box? Could you get out? (If not, close your eyes and imagine a way to get out. You could open up a door or build some stairs.)

Your Seven Parts

Imagine that there are seven parts of yourself.

List the parts:

1 _____

2 _____

3 _____

4 _____

5 _____

6 _____

7 _____

If one part were missing, which one would it be? _____

Where could you find it? _____

The High Priestess says:
Harmony, balance and integration will come to you through:

_____

Definition

We are comprised of many different aspects and sometimes, like Osiris, we may become scattered. This exercise will help you to clarify your sense of who you are and how to integrate the different facets of yourself.

Looking at...

The Facilitator

This is an exercise to help you develop the powers of your inner mind to solve problems and gain insights to fit all the fragments of your ideas and experiences together.

rite down a problem or situation that has been bothering you._____

Imagine that there is a person or a mythical being who is able to give you the perfect solution to the situation you listed above.

What is the name of this being?_____

What does he or she look like?_____

What is he or she wearing?_____

Try to describe this being more fully._____

Now ask for the solution to your problem.

What is the solution?_____

What further advice is there for you concerning the best way for you to proceed?_____

Definition

Whenever you face a difficult dilemma, use the image of the facilitator to find answers and discover solutions you thought you didn't have.

Another aspect of the symbolism of the High Priestess may be seen in the following folktale.

The Story of the Hedly Kow

nce upon a time there was an old woman who lived on the edge of a forest. She earned her living by doing errands and odd jobs for the nearby farmers and villagers. She usually had only enough money to buy some bread and cheese for her supper, but she was a cheerful soul, without a care in the world. Every day she would get up early to gather pine cones and branches for her evening fire. Then she would set out to look for work. Her cottage was poor and old, but the old woman didn't mind; she was contented with her life.

The farmer's wives made sure that the old woman was on her way home long before dark, because after nightfall the Hedley Kow, a hobgoblin, was known to haunt the roads. All the villagers knew about him and they were all afraid of him. He could change his shape, and frighten the people out of their wits. He liked to chase them home and trick them with mean pranks.

One summer evening at almost dusk, the old woman was still on the road, hastening toward home. On the side of the road she saw a big black pot. The old woman wondered who would leave such a fine pot on the road, so she went over to examine it. "Maybe it has a hole in it and someone threw it out, but I could find a use for it myself, " she said as she looked inside.

"Oh glory!" she exclaimed when she peered into the pot. "It is filled with gold coins!" For awhile she just stood and gazed at her find, admiring the sparkle and shine of her treasure. "What a lucky person I am," she said to herself, and she pulled the pot to see how heavy it was. Then she decided that the only way she could manage to get such a heavy load home with her was to tie one end of her shawl to it, and drag it along the road. "I can think about what to do with my fortune all night long as I drag it home," the old woman mused, as she pulled and tugged the heavy pot along.

The old woman found a pot filled with gold coins.

"I could buy a grand new house or I could keep some gold coins on the mantle by the fireplace. I could bury the treasure at the foot of the garden." By this time, the old woman was growing tired from dragging the pot, so she stopped to take a rest.

However, when she peeked into the pot to look at her treasure, she found no gold in it. In its place was a shining lump of silver. In disbelief, she checked the pot again, but there was still a great lump of silver inside.

"I could have sworn there was gold in this pot when I found it, but I must have been dreaming," the old woman thought. "Well, maybe this is better anyway. Gold pieces are hard to keep safe. This will be easier to keep and I am still a rich woman. Oh but I am the lucky one!"

So the old woman continued her trudge homeward, cheerfully thinking of all the things she could do with her fine lump of silver.

The old woman dragged the heavy pot down the road.

Before long she became tired again from dragging the heavy pot, so the old woman stopped to rest. Once again, she checked inside of the pot to look at her treasure, but this time she was astonished to find that the silver was gone and in its place was a lump of lead.
"Mercy me!" the old woman exclaimed. Then, after a moment's thought, she said to herself, "Well this is a convenient turn of luck. I will have no trouble selling this lead, and I will have a lot of pennies for it! Now I won't have to stay awake nights worrying about being robbed of my gold or silver."

The old woman continued her slow journey along the road, dragging the pot behind her and chuckling over her good luck. Soon she stopped to rest again, by the side of the road. This time when she checked the pot, she found that her lump of lead had vanished, and in its place was a large stone. "My, my," the old woman exclaimed. After a moment she said to herself, "This is indeed a piece of luck! This is just the size stone I have been looking for, to keep my door open while I bring in the wood for my fire. I am a lucky woman!"

So she dragged her pot down the road, thinking about how well her stone would work as a door stop. When she finally reached her door, she bent her stiff back to pick up the stone, when all of a sudden the stone gave a squeal! Arms and legs and large ears appeared and when a creature finally emerged, he laughed and pointed his finger, making ugly faces at her as he danced around the old woman's small room.

The old woman stared at the creature in amazement. "Well well", she exclaimed. "If I'm not the luckiest old woman! Imagine, the Hedley Kow in my own house!"

The Hedley Kow emerged from the pot, pointing his finger and making ugly faces at the old woman.

The little man stopped short. "Do you mean to tell me that you are not afraid of the Hedley Kow?" he asked her.

"Oh no, I am not afraid of you," the old woman replied. "You are a rare sight to see, and besides you have done me no harm." She wrapped her shawl around her shoulders and nodded her head. "Good evening to you," she said and she went to the fireplace to fix her tea.

The little man turned around dejectedly, scratching his white beard as he walked out the door.

"Now," the old woman called to him as he left, "I don't have much, but you are welcome to share some bread and cheese and a cup of good hot tea, if you would like to join me for supper."

As the two sat down to eat, the little bit of cheese became a fine large block, and there appeared some fresh fruit and a fresh loaf of sweet brown bread. The two had a cheerful meal and after they ate their fill, they sat comfortably by the fire. The Hedley Kow entertained the old woman with stories of his pranks and adventures until tears ran down the old woman's cheeks. "I have never had such a fine evening as this has been," she said to the Hedley Kow.

After that, the Hedley Kow came to join the old woman for supper and to visit quite often. And the old woman found that her woodpile was always full and that her cupboard was never empty. But she wisely said nothing about her new friend to her neighbors.

When the village folk would curse the Hedley Kow for his mischief, the old woman would merely say, "Oh, he isn't so bad, he just likes to stir up some mischief from time to time."

In this story, the old woman was not afraid of the hidden parts of her psyche, or her unconscious self, which is represented by the contents of the pot and the hobgoblin. Instead, she was trustful and welcoming of whatever should appear, not judging its apparent material worth, but accepting it on its own merits. As a result, all of her needs were met and she was happy and contented, living in harmony between the inner and the outer worlds, the black and the white pillar of the High Priestess, or in this case, the Hedley Kow and the village folk.

The Realms of the Unconscious

 he symbolism of the High Priestess reveals to us that by examining our lives in terms of our inward needs, we can take into account the symbolic dimensions of our minds.

Now that the neurophysiologists have discovered that one half of the human brain is predisposed to thinking in intuitive, spontaneous and sensory terms, we have become more able to accept that type of process as authentic. Once we have established that there is indeed one half of the brain that thinks in metaphors and symbols, we are free to acknowledge the existence of that world where poetry, music, art and feelings are more important than money and machinery.

In following chapters we will explore various methods of tapping the processes of the right hemisphere. We can reach beyond our limitations into dimensions which connect us with the cosmos, that essence of life the Eastern mystics and the Western spiritualists have always known about, where the cosmic and the human become one.

In the past, myths played the part that counselors, therapists and psychologists, or psychiatrists do today.

Otto Rank said, "The role of psychology is to serve modern man until there is some new point of view that will help us find believable and liveable meaning in our lives, which have lost a sense of meaningfulness."

We will be able to achieve this sense of meaning and wholeness when we learn to unite the two sides of the brain in a harmonious balance.

The High Priestess represents the long dormant processes of the creative, idealistic, poetic part of ourselves. This is the domain of the artist and the poet, and this side we have neglected. And yet these are the attributes which can lead us to the discovery of a sense of purpose and fulfillment.

The message of the High Priestess is that we need to rediscover our ability to dream and to feel. The two pillars are the doorway to the psyche, whose language is not made of words. It speaks through the medium of images, metaphors and dreams. In order to listen to our inner wisdom, we must discover and understand these images; these are the images that are loaded with significance. This is the meaning that brings us direction, satisfaction and fulfillment.

Alfred Adler said that we know more than we understand. Our powers to think and analyze lag far behind our intuitive powers.

When we learn to trust our intuitive images, they will guide us safely through the trials of life.

The angel with a wreath is a symbol of victory.

Chapter 4
The Empress

The Empress

he Empress is the mother goddess. She is Demeter, the source of ideas and images from the springs of the unconscious mind. It was she who gave humankind the gift of wheat. She showed us how to plant the seed, cultivate, and finally harvest the wheat and grind it.

She represents mother nature, with whom we must come to terms. We have come into her domain where she can teach us many things, if we have the wisdom to listen to her.

The Empress

In the field of blooming and fragrant violets and lilies, ivy and lilacs, wheat and blossoming pomegranate trees, grasses ripple and the birds are singing. The hives of the bees are alive with springtime; the trees whisper and the river murmurs in the living joy of nature.

The Empress sits on her flowering throne with a crown of greenery on her head. Behind her there are two snow-white wings. She holds a scepter in her hand.

She says to you, I send you along the stream past the flowers and the wheat fields, through the forest of many trees, in search of:

_____

Which you will find in the_____

I am clothed by the sun, and the moon is beneath my feet.

I am_____

I can_____

I will_____

I have_____

Now the Empress smiles and opens her arms to you.

She says_____

The Mother Goddess represents nature and the instinctive part of your psyche. She is the mother of your intuition and creative imagination.

What guidance and inspiration does she have for you?

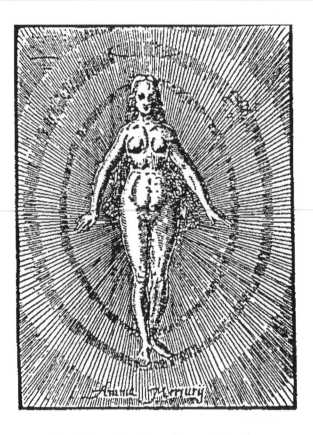

The Anima Mundi, or the world mother.

Affirmation

Say to yourself:
I have a blossoming garden of creative potential which is nurtured to fruition for my highest personal fulfillment.

This exercise is useful whenever you are troubled by events beyond your control. It can also help you overcome stress by helping you let go of your anxieties and emotional burdens.

Looking at…

The Ancient Altar

lose your eyes and relax your body and your mind. Imagine you are standing in front of a fire which is burning at an ancient altar.

See yourself pick up several leaves from the ground. On each leaf is the name of something that has been bothering you.

Write down the names of the leaves

_____   _____

_____   _____

Take the leaves, one by one, and throw them into the fire.

Watch as each leaf burns and turns to smoke.

Watch the smoke rise and float off into the sky, taking your problems with it.

Looking at...

The Locket

Imagine you have come across a heart-shaped locket.

*What is is made of?*_____

*What is inside?*_____

*How do you feel about the locket?*_____

*What will you do with it?*_____

*Write in the name that belongs in the center of the heart.*_____

Definition

The heart represents the wisdom of feeling, of following one's heart rather than the wisdom of rational knowing. The heart represents compassion, understanding, love and charity.

Is your heart made of something valuable? The things inside represent the feelings you treasure.

The Myth of Cybele, The Great Mother

 t is told that the Great Mother Goddess was born in Phrygia. In ancient times, Meion became king of Phrygia and Lydia. He married Dindyme, who gave birth to an infant daughter. The king was furious to have a daughter instead of a son, so he abandoned the infant to be exposed to the elements and perish on Mt. Cybelus.

However, the leopards and other ferocious beasts found the infant and protected her.

The ferocious beasts kept Cybele safe from harm.

The shepherd women who tended their flocks on the mountain were astonished to see the baby girl, who was taken care of by the beasts, and they called her Cybele, after the mountain.

The child grew to be strong and beautiful, and as she grew she came to be admired for her intelligence. She was the first to devise the pipe of many reeds and it was she who invented the cymbals and the kettle-drums, which accompany the games and the dance. In addition, she taught the people how to heal the sickness of both the flocks and the children, by means of rites and purification.

Cybele saved babies from death by her spells. Her devotion and her love led all the people to revere her and call her the Mother of the Mountain.

The Song of the Goddess

I am she that is the natural mother of all things, mistress and governess of all the elements, the initial progeny of worlds, chief of the powers divine, queen of all that are in hell, the principal of them that dwell in heaven, manifested alone and under one form in all the gods and goddesses. At my will the planets of the sky, the wholesome winds of the seas, and the lamentable silences of hell be disposed; my name, my divinity is adored throughout the world, in divers manners, in variable customs, and by many names. For the Phrygians that are the first of all men call me the Mother of the gods of Pessinus; the Athenians, which are sprung from their own soil, Cecropian Minerva; the Cyprians, which are girt about by the sea, Paphian Venus; the

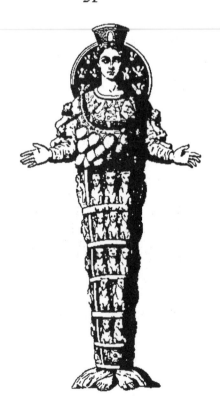

Cretans which bear arrows, Dictynian Diana; the Sicilians, which speak three tongues, infernal Proserpine; the Eleusians, their ancient goddess Ceres; some Juno, others Bellona; others Hecate; others Rhamnusia, and principally both sorts of the Ethopians, which dwell in the Orient and are enlightened by the morning rays of the sun, and the Egyptians, which are excellent in all kinds of ancient doctrine, and by their proper ceremonies accustomed to worship me, do call me by my true name, Queen Isis. Behold I am come to take pity on thy fortune and tribulation.

(Apuleus, The Golden Ass)

The goddess depicted as the mother and queen of all things.

The Myth of the Mother Goddess

emeter, the great mother goddess, had a daughter named Persephone, the maiden of spring.

One day, Persephone strayed too far when she was picking flowers in a meadow with her companions. The lord of the dark underworld, the king of the dead, carried her away in his chariot.

When Demeter learned of the abduction of her beloved daughter, she searched all over the land for her. Finally, she learned that Persephone was under the earth, among the shadowy dead.

Demeter mourned for her lost daughter and in her great sorrow she withdrew her powers from all the crops, and the earth became barren. Nothing on the earth grew; no seed sprang up and there was winter. The goddess refused to let the earth bear fruit until she had seen her daughter.

After many complaints from the gods, Zeus sent his messenger into the underworld to get Persephone back. But the lord of the underworld had persuaded Persephone to eat a pomegranate seed, knowing that if she did she must return to him.

Demeter was filled with joy at the return of her daughter, and she made the fields rich with abundant harvests.

But for four months every year, Demeter loses her daughter to the lord of the underworld. And during this time the world is barren, as the goddess mourns.

Demeter, with sheaves of wheat, pomegranates, and a bee hive.

Reflections...

Without the emergence of ideas from the subconscious, we are left to a barren winter of our own despair. In the inevitable cycle of life, there are times when we feel abandoned and we grieve until the return of the lost parts of ourselves from the underworld, or the inner mind, whereupon we become revitalized. We can then once again rediscover the sources of our joy and inspiration, and life is born anew.

Messages from the Underworld of the Mind

 he unconscious is the underworld, the source of our images. Without them, life is bleak and barren, but the uninspired time of our winter is a necessary period of struggle before the reawakening, or springtime of new ideas.

The world in which we live is filled with stimulation. We are constantly being bombarded by sound, color and action. Even in our inactive moments we provide ourselves with the stimuli of TV, radio, records and movies, as well as incessant internal chatter. Seldom do we shut out this outer world to listen to the world inside.

It is possible, and it is important for us to learn to quiet the noise and constant demands of the external world. Meditation, for example, is an ancient method for concentration on the quiet within. When we learn to silence the outside noise, we can discover the richness deep inside.

When the external world has been quieted, we can turn to the art of visualization. Visualizing can have remarkable power over many aspects of our lives.

Visualizing mental pictures has been shown to be at least as significant as any outer form of experience. A classic example of this is an experiment which has been widely quoted (from Research Quarterly by Alan Richardson), on the effects of mental practice on improving skills for sinking basketballs.

A test group of students practiced shooting baskets every day for 20 days, and were scored on the first and last days. A second group was scored on the first and last days, but they engaged in no basketball practice during the 20 test days. A third group was scored on the first day. Then for the 20 test days, they spent 20 minutes a day *imagining* they were shooting baskets. If they missed, they would readjust their aim and try again (in their imagination only). The first group which had actually practiced, scored an improvement of 24 percent. The second group, with no practice, showed no improvement. The third group, which had practiced in their imagination only, scored an improvement of 23 percent!

This illustrates that mental pictures, mental exercise, can be as powerful and effective as the actual physical experience itself.

Physiologists who have studied the brain have discovered that there is actual physical change when a person sitting in a laboratory visualizes a frightening object. Likewise, when a person imagines something soothing, the body responds; the heart rate lowers, there is a decrease in blood pressure and all the muscles relax.

Visualizing

 t is easy to learn the techniques of visualization by learning to focus the mind on an imagined object. As we visualize something we begin to identify with it just as if it had been an actual experience. Thus we can visualize a desired goal (as the basketball shooters did) and actually mentally become part of the picture. For example, if you want to give a lecture and you feel anxious about it, you can visualize yourself delivering a brilliant talk. This visualization will become a part of your own personal history. Then when you give the actual talk, it feels familiar and is a much less threatening experience because you have the confidence of having already performed the task successfully.

Once you have visualized yourself performing effectively, the experience becomes part of your background, a successful history on which to draw for future use.

Imagery and visualization techniques have been used throughout history as effective tools for healing. Visualization is used by shamans to create harmony in the sick person and reunite him with his soul. The technique was used in Hermetic Philosophy to cure disease by visualizing perfect health. The ancient Greeks had their patients dream of being healed by the gods.

Mary Baker Eddy developed the Church of Christian Science, in which she saw God as the infinite divine mind, which could heal all illness. "When fear disappears" she said, "the foundation of disease is gone."

Relaxation and visualization are gaining respect as methods for treating disease today. We have begun to discover broad uses of visualization and imagery for all aspects of life, whether we are sick or simply want to enrich the quality of our everyday experiences and to increase our ability to understand our lives.

Through visualization we can reach past the barriers that separate us from the deepest parts of ourselves, to open up the sources of power and healing that will take us beyond the limits of the material world.

This is the message of The Empress.

The Empress is the mother of ideas and images from the unconscious.

Chapter 5
The Emperor

The Emperor

The Emperor represents the masculine, paternalistic aspect of the psyche, the father who rules the world from his throne. He wears a crown on his head, the symbol of his dominion. He represents the powers of reason, regulation, and order.

The Emperor upholds the status quo. He is a practical and powerful administrator of the material world and he regulates life by his law.

Looking at…

The Emperor

You have entered the land of the empire. The emperor's castle lies past the long road and across the deep castle moat. A password has been given to you which will allow you to travel safely into the realms of the emperor.

To visit the castle you must travel past the guards until you reach the castle itself. Here you are escorted into the emperor's audience chamber.

The emperor is sitting on his throne beside a huge blazing fire. He wears a golden crown and the sign of an eagle is on his shield. He holds a sceptre, the symbol of his great power.

The emperor says to you, "I am the great principles; I am action, I am completion, and I am result; I am the great law."

The emperor says to you:

I am _____

I have _____

I will _____

I always _____

My message for you is _____

Your password is _____

With this password you can _____

Definition

The Emperor is the king; he is the father figure who rules as a powerful but benevolent dictator.   He represents confidence, assertion, authority and achievement.

The message and password are your own manifestations of confidence, authority and achievement.

Affirmation

Say to yourself:
I have will and power, discipline and ambition to meet all
of my highest goals.

Looking at...

The Sword

*I*magine there is an old sword on the road in front of you.

*What does the sword look like?*_____

*How do you feel about it?*_____

*What will you do with it?*_____

*Where did it come from?*_____

*To whom does it belong?*_____

*What color is it?*_____

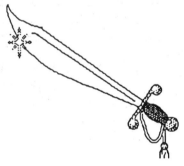

Definition

The sword is a symbol of power, strength, courage, authority and leadership. What do your answers to the exercise of the sword indicate to you about your feelings about these attributes? Are you comfortable with the sword? Does it belong to you? If not, close your eyes and imagine the sword with your name engraved on the hilt; it is your own symbol of power and strength, and you are armed with it as you travel the mysterious roads ahead.

Looking at...

The Crown

You have come across a crown along the path.

What does it look like?

_____

What is it made of?

_____

How do you feel about it?

_____

What will you do with it?

_____

To whom does it belong?

_____

Definition

The crown represents victory, dignity, sovereignty and reward, the highest attainment. Did you put it on? If not, what have you learned about your feelings about success? Close your eyes and imagine you are wearing the crown... feel your power.

The Throne

You have come to a great throne. You climb up to it and sit down.

How do you feel? _____

What do you do? _____

Definition

The throne is the seat of authority, knowledge and rule.
Are you comfortable sitting there? If not, spend a few
minutes imagining yourself sitting on a throne that was
made especially for you, with your initials inscribed on it.
As you sit on it you have a sense of great strength; you
are able to tap your unlimited power.

Order and Reason

he great Greek god Zeus was the protector, the ruler and the representative of the Olympic order. His rule was absolute over gods and men.

Like Zeus, the Emperor represents law and order, authority and paternity over the material world. He is still very much with us and his rule affects our society even today.

We are all familiar with the authoritative rule of the system, which, in its excess, is suspicious of independent, creative innovation and favors conformity to the prevailing order.

What can we learn from the Emperor? We know his powers and we also see his excesses; in fact they may be our own. We all subject ourselves to rules, schedules, and calendars, sometimes at the expense of our spontaneity and our creativity, and sometimes even our humanity.

The Emperor represents personal power, but he also stands as a warning against creating a world in which all reality is regulated and all truth is measurable, tangible and quantitative.

An understanding of the necessity for limiting the powers of the Emperor can be seen in the following quote from Laozus Tao and Wu Wei, in which the ruler is cautioned to avoid arrogance, and to be flexible, as well as to avoid violence.

When a magistrate follows the Tao he has no need to resort to force of arms to strengthen the Empire, because his business methods alone will show good returns. Briars and thorns grow rank where an army camps. But harvests are the sequence of a great war. The good ruler will be resolute, and then stop, he dare not take by force. One should be resolute, but not boastful; resolute but not arrogant; resolute but yielding when it cannot be avoided; resolute but he must not resort to violence. With a resort to force, things flourish for a time, but then decay.

The Emperor and the Ego

ur personal interpretations of our experiences constitute authoritative messages which are accepted without reservation by the passive subconscious mind. Thus, in a sense each of us is the Emperor. We make our own laws, define our own realities and then find ourselves acting within the constrains of our interpretations of reality.

The authoritative aspect of the ego can be seen in the mythologic figure of Zeus, who may be in danger of becoming overwhelmed by his ego, as he attempts to force his will on every aspect of the environment. If we can shift our attention away from the ego, away from the confines of our absorption with the Self, which is our usual preoccupation when we are thinking in the literal mode ("How do I look? Do they like me? Am I more successful than he is?"), we suddenly open ourselves to a whole new world of meaning.

We are all searching for a sense of meaningfulness in our lives. Albert Einstein once asked, "What is the meaning of life? To find a satisfactory answer to that question," he said, "Is to become religious." The realm in which we will find answers in our search for meaningfulness must go beyond the literal and beyond the Self, and beyond the realms of the Emperor.

The emperor rules our world with authority and wisdom. He represents the powers of our culture in its scientific and technical splendor. But we can find our own truth only when we look inside.

The Soul Lost in the Age of Technology

I f we were to think of ourselves as nothing more than complicated super computers, we would ignore our inner lives, our meanings and our souls. When we assume that reality is what the advertisers say it is in the commercials or in the glossy ads, our framework of belief becomes focused on externals. There is less inside as we focus more energy on what goes on outside. Finally, we end up with no coherent overall sense of meaning or purpose in life, living in a vacuum in which everything is OK until the machines are turned off. Then, late at night, when we are all alone, we find ourselves face to face with the terrifying void. With no inner significance we are doomed to constantly grasp for external answers, which turn out to be merely illusions.

Inside ourselves is a realm which haunts our dreams and controls our lives in subtle ways, but we have left it unexplored. Maybe we are experts at the jobs we do during the day, but the hidden half of our minds, the inner workings, remain more mysterious than ever.

Some anthropologists tell us that without a fundamental sense of meaning, the human organism often does not fulfill its essential biological functions.

Among primitive tribes, people pray to a god of the lake or to a god of fertility, and they find meaning all around them. But if our only god is the coin of the realm, we will constantly feel disappointed and let down. The literal world has imprisoned our ability to dream, and life feels empty.

If we invest all our hopes and dreams in another person, another place, or another thing, we are invariably disappointed and disillusioned. Our personal salvation cannot come from another person, place or thing. Rather, a sense of salvation comes from our relationships with our inner selves, and it belongs to the world of the soul.

Chapter 6
The Hierophant

The Hierophant

he Hierophant represents the saintly, religious aspect of the psyche. He is the high priest, the rabbi or the pope. He sits between two columns holding a cross in his left hand. The keys are at his feet.

Looking at...

The Hierophant

The Great Master is sitting in the temple. He wears the robes of a spiritual leader. His face is serene and his eyes are penetrating as he looks at you. You feel the magnitude of his presence, you know this is truly a saintly man.

The Holy Man says to you, "Look for the path that leads inward; follow the truth and find the treasures from within."

The Hierophant says to you:

The first truth is _____

The miracle is _____

Your pathway leads to _____

The keys at the Hierophant's feet are from the sun and the moon. They can unlock _____

which is kept _____

Definition

> The Hierophant represents the blessings of intuitive guidance. The path is your way to self-fulfillment. The words of the Hierophant are messages to you from your own intuition.

Affirmation

Say to yourself:
I am guided and directed by my highest wisdom for the greatest good, in myself and in the world.

Looking at...

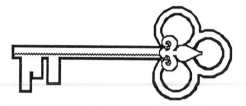

The Key

 magine that you have found an old key by the side of the road.

What does it look like? _____

How do you feel about it?

_____

Where did it come from? _____

To whom does it belong?
_____

What will it unlock? _____

What will you do with it? _____

Definition

The key symbolizes knowledge, so your impression of the key and your feelings about it reflect your feelings about knowledge.

Your response to the questions about where the key came from, what it unlocks, to whom it belongs, and what you will do with it, will give you some understanding of the role of wisdom in your life.

The Story of John-Baptist Vianney

 ohn Vianney was the son of a French peasant farmer. His studies for the priesthood were quite slow and unpromising, but eventually he was ordained, more because of his devoutness and his good will than for any other qualifications.

When he was finally ordained, he was sent out to a lonely and neglected village, as the parish priest. There he devoted his heart and soul to his parishioners. Soon, Father Vianney came to be known as a gifted preacher and confessor. Villagers from miles around began to talk about the country priest's gifts and powers.

Soon the isolated village became a place of pilgrimage for tens of thousands of people who came from all over France and beyond. For year after year Father Vianney spent up to eighteen hours a day in the confessional. He had extraordinary powers of insight and understanding. It was even said that he was able to tell about distant and future events.

Some of the other clergy complained to the Bishop about Father Vianney's work, calling him a madman and a charlatan. Finally, the bishop said to them, "I wish, gentlemen, that all my clergy had a touch of the same madness." [6]

Fr. Vianney had extraordinary powers of insight and understanding.

A popular early Christian tradition relates that at the moment an invading Turkish army entered the great Byzantine church of St. Sophia, there was a liturgy being celebrated.

The priest who held the holy sacrament saw the Muslim army rush into the church. Miraculously, the altar wall opened in front of him. He entered and disappeared within.

The tradition says that when Constantinople (or modern-day Istanbul) once again is in the hands of the Christians, the priest will come out from the altar wall and continue the liturgy. [7]

The priest, or Hierophant represents the link between God and man through the ritual creed and ceremony of formalized religion. The priest a guide in our striving for transcendent meaning; he is a symbol of our search for a connection with God, and an aid for making this connection.

The priest, or hierophant, represents a link between God and humankind.

The Opening in the Floor

 magine that there is an opening in the center of the floor in your room.

How deep is the hole?_____

How far down can you see?_____

Imagine you climb down through the hole._____

What do you see?_____

When you reach the bottom, what do you find?_____

(Finish the sentences)

I feel _____

I wish _____

I will _____

I need _____

I fear _____

I secretly _____

Imagine there is a hole in the floor…

Looking at...

The Opening in the Sky

 magine you look up and you see that there is an opening in the sky.

What do you see?_____

How do you feel about it? _____

How big is the hole?_____

You can see up through the opening. What lies beyond?_____

_____

Now picture yourself going up through the opening. How do you feel?

_____

What do you see?_____

When you have ascended, finish these sentences:

I feel _____

I am_____

I must_____

I have_____

I believe _____

Imagine you look up and see an opening in the sky...

Definition–The Opening in the Floor

The Opening in the Floor represents the descent into the unconscious. How do you feel about it? The way you feel will affect your willingness to explore your inner regions; the sentences you finished show your innermost feelings about your descent.

If you are uncomfortable or afraid of going down into the hole in the floor, imagine you go down again, this time knowing that there are great gifts and guidance is waiting for you and that you are safe and welcome.

Definition–The Opening in the Sky

The Opening in the Sky represents your spiritual vision, your ascent into the realms of God. The way you feel about this ascent reflects your sense of spirituality. It shows how you feel about God and spiritual transcendence.

If you are afraid of going up through the opening in the sky, imagine that your angel is with you, to guide and to show you the things that are in heaven.

The Vision

In the story about the priest at St. Sophia, the priest could not be overcome or destroyed. When external forms of the faith are invaded, the priest, who is our own striving for a connectedness with God, withdraws inward, into the altar, or into a sacred place within the self where it will remain, listening to the sounds of the inner voice, until it is safe, and free once again to act out the rituals and symbols of its faith.

It is the vision which can provide answers and solutions to make sense of our lives. The vision, which is the source of our inner quest, comes from intuition, not from literal outward manifestations. It is, rather, that dynamic image which we can accept and believe in wholeheartedly that can change even our most hopeless situations into important opportunities for growth and advancement.

Finding this vision and learning to follow it is the significance of the symbol of the Hierophant.

A vision that we believe in completely can change any situation into an opportunity for growth.

Carl Jung said that when we feel weak, the inner center will supply us with images that are right at any moment, to give us a sense of order and meaning.

The search for a sense of direction and purpose will lead us to the world of the psyche, which goes beyond words.

Going Beyond Words

The world that exists past our words is where images and symbols express the ineffable. By understanding these images, and interacting with them through techniques which use visualization and imagery, we can begin to identify and participate in all aspects of our lives in new, rich ways.

An experience which seems pointless when participated in on a literal level can become alive and important when we participate in it fully, when we look for its spiritual significance.

When we visualize an image rather than just looking at the object itself or at a picture, all of the symbolic content of that image becomes personal and at the same time universal. It comes to represent something about our own experience, it becomes a metaphor for some aspect of our lives.

When we view them literally, we may note that there are interesting recurring themes in fairy tales and myths. But when we are able to recognize these themes as metaphors for the life experiences we all share, they suddenly possess a personal and compelling significance. These are the stories of our dreams. By understanding them, we can begin to understand the inner complexities which determine who we are and how we will live.

This, too, is the power an image takes when it is internalized, which is what happens when we use our imagination to inwardly visualize a picture. The picture we imagine becomes a part of ourselves and part of our experience.

The techniques of visualization can be used effectively for making significant improvements in our lives. Visualization may be used, among other things, to:

· Enrich our personal understanding of ourselves and our needs
· Expand our limitations and boundaries
· Review and learn from past events
· Develop new strengths and abilities
· Enhance our creative and intuitive processes
· Create a sense of confidence and of being centered

Step II in Review

During Step II of your travels you met with four sages, who represent four different aspects of your own psyche; two feminine and two masculine. They have provided you with the information and insights of your initiation into the role of the hero of the quest.

Write out a short summary of the most important aspects of your experience so far.

Write down the most important feeling and insights you have gained from your travels through this second stage, your initiation.

Step III- Withdrawal

You have been initiated. You have met with the sages and you have learned from them.

Now you must withdraw within yourself, to find your center and your balance.

The next four chapters will lead you through the withdrawal portion of your pilgrimage.

Chapter 7
The Lovers

The Lovers

T he symbol of the lovers represents the harmony of the two sides, the right and the left, the male and female, the yin and the yang.

This image represents unity and the synthesis of opposites in compassionate, loving intimacy.

Looking at…

The Lovers

 he Lovers stand on the green hillside. Their love is both a sacrifice and a prayer through which the magic of existence is opened. They represent the unification and integration of opposites into the whole each lacks separately.

The woman gazes upward, where she gains inspiration.

She says, I am _____

I can _____

I have _____

I will _____

The man gazes at the woman. He says, The dark cloud between us represents _____

I will _____

The best way to reach the top of the mountain is by

_____

The message from the Angel of the Air is

_____

Definition

The lovers represent the coming together of opposites.

This can only happen when there is a recognition and a respect for duality, and a mutual cooperation. This is the agreement of the conscious and the subconscious minds.

What is the dark cloud, or the basis of difficulty in your own personal process of growth and synthesis?

The top of the mountain is the fulfillment of your effort. How can you get there?

What can you learn from the message from the Angel of the Air?

This image, or mandala, represents the ying/yang concept
of two opposites in one; light and dark, male and female,
summer and winter, life and death.

The male/female androgyne is a symbol of perfection and wholeness in the union of the male and female forces in which the opposites , heaven and earth, night and day, mother and father, are united.

Affirmation

Say to yourself:
I am in harmony and a state of balance with both the feminine and the masculine parts of myself, and with my consciousness and my unconscious. Therefore I find a harmonious balance within myself and with others.

Looking at...

The Circle and the Square

hat symbol or picture would represent a sense of the material world for you? Write it in the box.

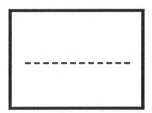

What would represent the spirit for you? Write it in the circle.

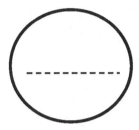

- - - - - - - - -

In your mind, imagine the merging of these two symbols. Try to hold the image.

*What does this new, combined image say to you?*_____

Balancing the material and the spiritual realms is the pathway to inner harmony.

Definition

This exercise will help you find a mental balance between the material and the spiritual realms. Use the message of the new, combined image when you feel the need to refocus.

Looking at...

I magine that you are looking into a magical mirror.

What do you see? _____

How do you feel about the image in the mirror? _____

Imagine that the mirror image finishes these sentences

I am _____

I can _____

I will _____

I must _____

I secretly _____

Definition

In dreams, a mirror often symbolizes the unconscious mind reflecting oneself in a new, unexpected way. In the Greek myth, the Gorgon Medusa could only be looked at through a mirror; looking at her directly would turn men to stone.

On the other hand, the reflection in the mirror can be seen to represent the manifest, temporal world. When we remove ourselves from this world of appearances, we will become free to explore the full dimensions of our real selves, instead of the limitations of our reflections.

The Mountain Top

magine that you have been climbing and finally you reach the top of a tall mountain.

*What do you see?*_____

*How do you feel?*_____

*What do you do?*_____

*What do you find?*_____

What can you see as you look over to the outer side of the mountain?

_____

The figure on the top of the mountain has achieved fulfillment with the help of the angel.

Definition

Ascent to the top of the mountain represents the attainment of the whole and unlimited from the partial, limited and unfulfilled. The other side of the mountain is the future.

The Myth of Eros and Psyche

 he Greek myth of Eros and Psyche is a metaphorical story of the two lovers, Eros, or love, and Psyche, or the soul. It is a variation of the beauty and the beast theme.

Psyche was the beautiful daughter of a king. She had two sisters but she was far more beautiful than they. However, her sisters each soon found husbands, while Psyche remained in her father's house, without suitors. The king, despairing of ever finding a husband for her, consulted an oracle. The oracle told him to abandon Psyche on the top of a mountain where she would be taken off by a monster. The king and queen were in anguish, but they had to obey this decree because they were told it was the will of the gods, whom they feared to disobey.

Actually, Aphrodite, the goddess of love, was jealous of Psyche and for revenge she ordered her own son, Eros, to make Psyche fall in love with a poor, ugly creature. But, when Eros saw Psyche, he fell in love with her himself.

Psyche was led to the mountain top to be abandoned, but instead of being taken away by a monster, the wind, Zephyrus, lifted Psyche gently off to a beautiful castle. Psyche was attended by invisible servants.

The wind carried Psyche to a beautiful castle.

Lovely voices waited on her and fed her and amused her by day. At night, in the darkness, the husband the oracle had told of joined her. He did not seem to be a monster, but Psyche could not see him.

Every morning her husband would fly away, to join her again the next night. Psyche was happy but lonely, so she persuaded her husband to allow her sisters to visit her. He warned her of the danger of her nostalgia but she begged and he finally agreed.

The wind Zephyrus brought Psyche's sisters to the palace. They were bitterly jealous to see the splendor of the palace where their sister lived and they convinced her to find out what her husband looked like. Unable to overcome her own curiosity, and at the insistence of her sisters, Psyche hid a knife and a lamp in her room to see and kill her monster husband.

But when Psyche saw her beautiful husband, she realized he was the god Eros. In her amazement and fright, she spilled a drop of boiling oil from her lamp on him. When he awoke he saw what she had done, and he flew off at once, never to return again.

Months passed. Psyche was broken hearted and she decided to find her husband. First she punished her sisters by telling them that Eros asked to see them. Delighted, they jumped off a cliff, thinking that Zephyrus the wind waited to carry them off. Instead they fell to the ravine below.

Psyche traveled throughout the whole world searching for Eros, but her efforts were in vain. Finally she went to Aphrodite, who tortured her and then sent her off to the underworld to bring back a box of beauty ointment. She was told not to open it, but she could not resist. When she opened it a sleep vapor escaped and she fell unconscious.

However, Eros was desperately in love with Psyche. When he saw her in the magic sleep he wakened her and went to Zeus himself to ask for permission to marry a mortal. Zeus gave his consent and finally Aphrodite and Psyche were reconciled. Later, Eros and Psyche had a beautiful child, whom they named Pleasure.

This story can be seen as a description of the soul, or Psyche, which is beautiful but corruptible, until it has undergone the tests which will make it worthy, aided by the power of love, or Eros.

The two lovers can be seen as the two different aspects of the self, the soul and the worldly outer person, which can be united as lovers after corruptions, pettinesses and vanities are overcome.

Dreams and Images

In dreams the psyche is fragmented into many parts. These various parts are connected by scenes and stories. We learn from dreams about the true nature of the psyche and the nature of psychic reality, which deals not in terms of I but of we, not of one but of many.

Dreams free us from our identity with the ego of the waking state, which is represented in the myth by Psyche's sisters. This freedom allows us to experience a greater truth than we are ever able to know when we are thinking rationally and literally. But our dreams are largely inaccessible. We often forget them or we are unable to understand them.

Any type of visual imagery has the same attendant sensations and effects as the actual situation, whether it is a dream or a waking visualization. Because our dreams are often difficult to remember and to understand, we can learn to use other kinds of images to uncover the hidden facets of the self.

Certain images and symbols have a great deal of meaning to our unconscious minds. They constitute the inner language, the primary language that exists before feelings are translated into words. By learning this language of symbols and images, we can establish a dialogue with the hidden part of ourselves we often ignore or misunderstand. Communicating with our unconscious minds can provide a powerful resource for defining and reaching our goals.

Visual imagery, imagining something and seeing it in the mind, can be a wonderful tool for controlling our moods and even our health. If we visualize something negative in our minds, the resulting mood and feelings will be negative. If, on the other hand, we visualize something positive, our disposition will be positive. By learning the techniques of visualization we can discover a great source of inner power, and a medium as rich as our dreams for self-understanding.

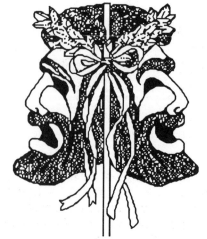

Obviously if one part of ourselves is aiming in one direction and the other, the hidden part, for reasons as inscrutable as our dreams, is heading off in the opposite direction, we will exist in a perpetual state of inner conflict.

If, however, our outer, rational functions and our inner intuitive impulses are in agreement about their mutual goals and objectives, we will have dramatically increased our prospects for success, happiness and health. With the whole system in agreement and striving for common objectives, a new strength and power will suddenly become available to us. And considering that there are billions of brain cells that are never used in the lifetime of even the most brilliant and accomplished human being, it is not at all unreasonable for us to expect that we can become capable of undreamed of accomplishments when we learn to communicate with our inner minds.

The king and the queen are in harmony. The eagle represents spiritual inspiration. The lions are the soul and the spirit.

The alchemical picture above portrays The Lovers, or the union of opposites, with two lions which symbolize the soul and the spirit. They must be united in their body; the soul and spirit must become one in the heart.

The hermaphrodite, or androgyne, also represents this conjunction, or this bringing together of opposites. The sun is male and the moon is female. Together they form a figure of perfection in whom the soul and spirit are merged into one.

When these opposites are brought together, the body (or material world) becomes spiritualized, and the spirit becomes expressed in solid practical terms, like morality and goodness.

This philosophical egg represents the union of the opposites, which triumphs over chaos and the dragon. The seven planets represent seven stages of transformation and seven aspects of the personality.

Chapter 8
The Chariot

The Chariot

he Chariot represents that part of the self whose power lies in self control and self discipline. It stands for victory over the instincts, mastery, conquest and triumph.

Looking at…

The Charioteer

he Charioteer stands ready; he is in control of himself and his life. He drives a team of two creatures.

Imagine yourself as the Charioteer.

What are the creatures that pull your chariot? _____

What is the direction of your efforts? _____

The Charioteer says: _____

My strength is _____

I am _____

I can _____

I have _____

My weakness is _____

I am hiding the _____

The direction I will take is _____

Definition

Plato described the soul as a winged chariot drawn by two horses representing contrary aspects of human nature, the one striving upward, the other pulling down.

The qualities of the driver are symbolized by the type of team driven; Freyja drives a chariot drawn by cats to represent a lunar and magical journey. White horses can represent spirituality and purity. The human-headed sphinx suggests the human spirit overcoming animal instincts, or the union of intellectual and physical powers.

*The wreath is a symbol
of glory and victory.*

Affirmation

Say to yourself:
By harnessing all my efforts toward my goal, I will be victorious.

The Mask

 *magine yourself wearing a mask.*

What does the mask look like? _____

How do you feel about the mask? _____

Do you want to take it off? _____ *Why?* _____

The mask says:

I am _____

I can _____

I will _____

I feel _____

I must _____

I have _____

Definition

The mask represents protection and concealment. Wearing the mask of a specific character can represent an identification with it, or a concealment of yourself behind it. Animal or bird masks represent communion with nature and instinctual wisdom.

The mask you wear may be an indication of your way of hiding from your problems, from yourself, or from the world. The message of the Charioteer is that you can triumph over adversity through self control and self discipline.

This visualization exercise uses the geometric symbol from Pythagoras' proof that the area of the square is equal to the area of two smaller squares built upon a right triangle, and vice versa. Symbolically this shows that the triangle is a perfect figure, because it contains and will support all that is built upon it.

Looking at...

The Three Boxes

Visualize three boxes, a small one, a medium sized one and a large one.

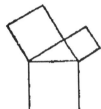

What color is the small box?_____

What color is the medium sized box?_____

What color is the large box?_____

Look into the small box. What do you find?_____

Imagine that the contents of the small box completes the following sentences:

I am_____

I wish_____

I must_____

I need_____

I feel_____

I secretly_____

Look in the medium-sized box.

What is inside?_____

Imagine that the contents of the medium-sized box completes the following sentences:

I am_____

I think_____

I wish_____

I need_____

I must_____

I feel_____

I secretly_____

What is inside the large box? _____

The contents of the large box completes the following sentences:

I am _____

I think _____

I wish _____

I must _____

I need _____

I feel _____

I secretly _____

Now imagine that the contents of all three boxes meet. What happens?

_____

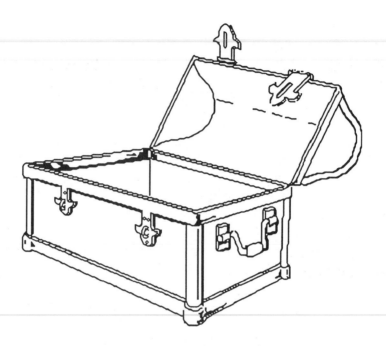

Definition

The small box represents the inner you. The middle box is your personality, the conscious you. And the large box represents your outer self, the public you. The relationship among these three images reflects the way these three parts of yourself interact.

If there were a conflict among the contents of the three boxes, close your eyes and imagine all the contents of the boxes together, and see them in a harmonious relationship.

The Myth of Theseus

 he ancient Greek hero, Theseus, who was the son of a queen and two fathers, a king and the god Poseidon, can be said to represent the charioteer. On one of his heroic exploits Theseus slew the monster Minotaur.

On the island of Crete, seven young boys and seven virgin girls were to be sacrificed as food for the Minotaur. Theseus set out to destroy the monster. When he arrived at Crete, princess Ariadne, the daughter of King Minos who was the ruler of the island, fell in love with him. Ariadne gave Theseus a ball of string so he could find his way back out of the labyrinth in which the Minotaur was kept. Theseus slew the beast and escaped the labyrinth. Then he left Crete, taking princess Ariadne with him, as well as her sister Phaedra.

But on the way home, Theseus abandoned Ariadne on the island of Naxos.

Before he had sailed off for Crete, Theseus had promised his father that he would put up a white flag if he had been successful in killing the Minotaur. If he failed, his ship would fly a black flag.

Theseus forgot his promise to change the black flag on the way home. Seeing the black flag, his father believed his son was dead. In his despair, he threw himself into the sea.

Theseus, like the Charioteer, was heroic in facing his task through his strength and courage. However, he abandoned Ariadne, and later, because of his thoughtlessness, his father killed himself.

This myth and the symbol of the Charioteer both seem to show us that strength and power are virtues which serve us in meeting the trials and adversities of life. But alone these virtues are not sufficient to ensure a fully victorious outcome. They must be tempered with other attributes, such as a respect for the feelings and needs of others, and a sense of integrity in personal relationships.

Freyja drives a chariot drawn by cats, which represent her inner powers.

Through the Labyrinth

Inner virtues and values which can guide the charioteer come from listening to the wisdom from within.

Theseus' guide out of the labyrinth was a simple ball of string. No type of weapon could have served him. The labyrinth is our own inner self and the Minotaur is all our negative thoughts and fears. We, like the hero, can slay our monsters, but only with the help of our inner, intuitive faculties.

When we return from the labyrinth, we will discover that we have glimpsed some unknown component that makes meaning possible, that turns empty events into important experiences and that gives our lives a new significance.

Unfortunately, however, once we are safely back from the labyrinth, we are often tempted to abandon those very processes which led us safely through, just as Theseus abandoned Ariadne.

The resources that guide us through the maze are the images, fantasies and symbols from the unconscious. Our conscious mind may try to define the experience we have inside the labyrinth, but words are a dim reflection of the actual experience. A whole non-verbal language exists in the unconscious. It is a visual language of form and symbol which uses shapes, colors and pictures instead of words.

Universal Symbols

ymbols are the nonverbal language of the unconscious mind. There are cultural symbols, such as a flag or a monument. And there are religious symbols, the cross and the Star of David, for example.

There are also what Carl Jung called universal symbols. These symbols will elicit the same response from any person no matter what culture he or she comes from. For instance, a dark cloud is a natural symbol suggesting all that we associate with a storm.

According to Jung, symbols are the basic universal language which is inherent in the structure of the human brain. Symbols are a part of our primal experience. Of course, the effect a symbol will have on someone will vary from person to person. It will also vary from one time to another, depending upon how you are feeling. But certain generalizations prevail which are consistent for anyone who views a universal symbol.

Color is one important form of symbolism. Each color represents certain attitudes and feelings, and will elicit particular responses. In fact, color has been observed to cause actual physiological changes in people. When one is exposed to the color red, for instance, the blood pressure, electrical conductance of the skin, respiration rate, eye blinks and brain wave patterns increase. On the other hand, when one is exposed to the color blue, the body becomes relaxed and tranquil.

Symbols and images are our only meaningful means of expression for inner experiences. We can attempt to translate them into words, but in order to completely understand our feelings we must be able to retain a memory of the image.

This is the reason that poetry and mythology, which utilize metaphors, symbolism and imagery, can be so moving for us. If we tried to interpret them as fact, whether historical, biographical or literal, their meaning would be diluted. The only way to understand images is by seeking their meaning intuitively.

We use symbols for many things that go beyond the range of human understanding. They represent concepts we cannot quite define or fully comprehend. The symbol is a picture which bridges the outer world and the inner.

In the world of symbols, the specific represents the universal. Things like a feeling of rebirth, or the idea of the meaning of life, or fate, are concepts we all understand and share but they do not fit into any rational system. They cannot be pinned down. They can only be understood symbolically.

The symbol serves to unify fragmented ideas and feelings and it allows us to have a glimpse of things that we could never otherwise understand.

In many ancient cultures the people saw spirit gods in the rivers and trees. They prayed to the spirits, and they depicted their visions of the gods in drawings and sculptures. They were close to nature and to creative expression, and they were accustomed to acting out their symbolic realities. Theirs was a world in which the powers of nature and the powers of prayer were vital parts of everyday life. The seasons and the rituals connected with them gave the people a sense of their place in the scheme of things and they experienced a harmony between the inner and the outer worlds. This is the balance we are missing. We have learned to manipulate the outer world, but we have abandoned the inner world in the process.

The subconscious mind is passive, but it is powerful. It can make us sick or cure us. It can make us rich or destroy us; we are angels or devils depending on the state of our unconscious minds. This is why it is so important that we learn its language, because in order for it to work on our behalf, we must communicate our wishes to the unconscious, which will then give us control of ourselves and thus our lives.

Once in control, we can take charge of the vehicle of our being to guide ourselves through the experiences of existence.

The driver of the chariot represents the mind or spirit directing the body through life. Its message is that instead of being tossed about by life, we can learn to master it.

Chapter 9
Strength

he symbol of Strength represents the vital energy of the higher self. This strength comes from using the positive energy of the spirit, which has the power to overcome our lower impulses.

Strength

he lion is subdued by the woman. She has the strength to endure despite all obstacles; she has the determination, the stamina, the courage and the energy to succeed.

She represents freedom from repression through perseverance and vitality. She has a passionate enthusiasm for life.

The woman who subdues the lion looks at you and you are infused with a vigorous sense of your own power and strength.

She asks you to write down a difficulty or a problem that has been of concern to you:

_____

Then she says: The lion can be controlled by _____

She says to you: you can _____

You must _____

You are _____

You will _____

Her warning is that _____

She says you will solve your difficulty by _____

She tells you to remember _____

Her power over the lion comes from her _____

Definition

The woman uses her love of life as her source of strength. This gives her the will to succeed.

She has harnessed the power of the beast, so it is no longer a threat to her. She has learned to assimilate that power and use it as her own.

The lion represents the drive for power
which we can learn to convert into
spiritual energy.

Affirmation

Say to yourself:
I release the energy from my greatest fears, weaknesses and repressions, and utilize it as a source of vitality and power, which enables me to reach my highest dreams.

Looking at...

Ways of Looking

Look outside, and find a tree.

Look at the tree as a botanical specimen. Think of it in terms of its categories; is it evergreen or deciduous, young or old, strong or weak? Is it larger or smaller than others you have seen of its kind? How does it compare with the other trees around it?

Describe the tree _____

_____

Close your eyes. Then look back at the tree again, but this time look at it as though you had never seen a tree before. Notice the way the light shines on its leaves, and how they move in the wind. See the colors and shapes of the tree and try to perceive it directly, emotionally, allowing yourself to experience your feelings about the tree. Pretend for a moment that you are the tree, feel a tree-knowingness throughout your mind and body.

Describe the tree the way it looks to you now _____

_____

Looking at...

Two Ways of Seeing

The next time you are in a grocery store, think about your shopping list and concentrate on the items you have come to the store to buy. Examine the objects you need, comparing ingredients and quantities listed on the labels. Think about the packaging — does it effectively represent the product? Think about the relative prices and which product is the best value.

Close your eyes and pause for a moment. Now try to imagine the store as a whole. Open your eyes and look at the light as it penetrates the aisles. Notice the temperature of the room. Become aware of the smells around you. Look at the colors and textures of the boxes, packages and the produce. Listen to the sounds — the people, the background music, the machinery, the intercom system. Feel the environment, become a part of it.

Now separate yourself from the surroundings.

Compare the two experiences.

Definition

Anything you do in life can be goal-oriented and fact-centered, or it can be a sensory stimulation. Try the two modes of perception the next time you are in a crowd of people, or at the zoo, or when you are out in nature. With practice you can learn to decide at will which mode to use and to select the one best suited to the moment, instead of being trapped into a half-awareness using only one part of your faculties.

Look for the beauty all around you and the beauty will become a part of you.

Looking at…

The Eye

Sit in a relaxed position, breathing evenly.

Close your eyes and imagine there is an eye in the middle of your forehead. Picture the eye clearly.

The eye says to you:

I am _____

I can _____

I will _____

I see _____

I remember _____

I secretly _____

I know _____

Definition

The Eye represents the faculty of intuitive vision, enlightenment and omniscience.

Looking at...

Imagine that a lion stands before you.

It says:_____

Then it tells you:

I am _____

I will_____

I can _____

I always _____

I must _____

How do you feel about the lion?_____

Definition

The Lion represents strength and power, which can be utilized for personal growth.

The Story of Molly Whuppie

nce there was a man and his wife who had so many children they could not feed them all. So the man took his three youngest daughters into the deep forest and left them there.

The girls wandered through the woods all night until they saw the lights of a house ahead. They went to the house and asked if they could stay the night.

The woman of the house told the children that she could not let them stay because her husband was a giant, and he would kill them if he found them. But the girls were so tired they begged her, "please let us stay and rest, we can leave before the giant gets home."

So the woman let them in and sat them down before the great fire with some bread and milk. Just as they sat down, the giant arrived at the door. "Fee fie fo fum, I smell the blood of an earthly one," the giant bellowed.

"It is just three homeless girls, let them stay the night," the wife pleaded. Finally the giant agreed.

The giant had his supper and then he told the three girls that they were to share a bed with his own three daughters. Before bed, he tied a straw rope around the neck of each of the three homeless children and he put a gold chain around the neck of each of his own daughters.

The youngest child, who was called Molly Whuppie, felt uneasy about the rope around her neck and the necks of her sisters, so she stayed awake when the rest fell asleep. When all the house was quiet, she took off the straw ropes and put them on the giant's daughters, and put the gold chains on herself and her sisters. Then she lay down again.

Late in the night, the giant rose and took the girls with the ropes around their necks and beat them to death. Molly woke her sisters and they ran back into the woods as fast as they could. Soon they saw a large castle where they asked permission to stay.

Molly told the king about her adventure with the giant and the king said, "Molly, you are a clever girl. If you go back and bring me the giant's magic sword, your eldest sister shall wed my eldest son."

"I will try," Molly said. So she went back to the giant's house and silently stole his sword. But the giant awoke and chased her through the forest. Molly ran until she reached the Bridge of One Hair. She ran over it but the giant was too big and he could not follow.

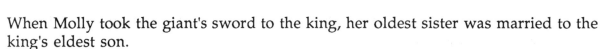

When Molly took the giant's sword to the king, her oldest sister was married to the king's eldest son.

Then the king said, "Molly, you are a clever girl, If you go back to the giant's house and bring me his purse of gold, your middle sister will marry my middle son."

"I will try," said Molly. Then she returned to the giant's house and while he was sound asleep, she stole his purse of gold. But before she could escape, he awoke and chased her through the forest until she reached the Bridge of One Hair. Molly crossed, but the giant was too big and he could not follow.

When she gave the king the giant's purse of gold, he said, "Molly, you are a clever girl. If you can get the giant's ring from his finger, you will wed my youngest son."

"I will try," said Molly. She returned once again to the giant's house, and when he was sound asleep she pulled his ring from his finger. But the giant awoke and caught her.

"What would you do if you caught a thief stealing your ring?", he asked Molly. Clever Molly answered, "I would put him in a sack with the cat and dog and hang him on a hook while I went to the woods to find a club. Then I would beat him with it."

"And that is just what I will do with you!" he exclaimed. He put Molly in a sack with the cat and the dog and he hung her on a hook and left to find a club.

While he was gone, Molly sang out, "Oh this is so pretty!"

The giant's wife begged Molly to show her what was so pretty, so Molly told her to cut a hole and climb in. As the wife climbed in, Molly climbed out. Then she sewed up the hole in the sack, and she hid behind the door.

Soon the giant returned with a huge club. He hit the sack and his wife yelled out "Stop it! It's me in here!" But the cat and dog made so much noise the giant could not hear her.

Then Molly, who did not want the giant to seriously hurt the woman, stepped out from behind the door. The giant chased her to the Bridge of One Hair. Molly crossed, but the giant was too big and he could not follow.

When she returned to the castle, Molly and the youngest prince were married. Molly never saw the giant again.

In this story, Molly's strength and courage enable her to overcome the giant, or the primitive animal nature in herself (or in humankind). She takes the giant's sword, his coins and his ring – the magical sources of his power, which she will transform into positive energy for her own use. The girl is not destroyed by the giant, instead she finds methods for utilizing his resources in new, positive ways for her own life.

The symbol of Strength represents the sacrifices of the ego, and self-awareness – which becomes lust, greed and other primitive drives, for spiritual inner forces which can be liberating and powerful.

The capacities of the spirit will help us tame the lower animal instincts which rule us. The lion represents the passionate devouring drive for power. When this drive is material instead of spiritual, it becomes destructive.

The demons in this illustration represent the lower animal instincts, or the 7 deadly sins (which are, anger, avarice, envy, gluttony, pride, lust and sloth).

In the picture below, the lion is devouring the sun. This symbolizes the violent passions which can overwhelm the consciousness. When the drive for power (the lion) focuses on a materialistic level, its force is corrupted. It becomes a vice and therefore destructive. But when the passion is spiritual, this symbol represents personal transformation and resurrection.

This is the chapter of Strength, in which the devouring energy of the lion is overcome and used as a vital positive energy for life.

The lion devouring the sun represents the consciousness of the self which can overwhelm violent desires.

Using Words to Distance Ourselves from the World

n the picture of Strength at the beginning of this chapter, the woman uses her spiritual, or inner resources to come to terms with her own lower impulses. She does not seek to destroy these impulses, but rather she will subdue them and learn to convert their power in order to use it for higher purposes of her own. She can do this through the powers of her spiritual nature, by feeling and experiencing life directly, without attempting to analyze or to manipulate it.

This is the process that belongs to the world of creativity and inspiration, where the viewer and the object somehow blend. This is the experience we have when we imagine, or visualize something, and the thing we see or visualize becomes a part of ourselves.

In many religions, images and meditation are used as ways to identify with and experience a sense of union with the divinity; to experience God as a living force from within, rather than as an external illusion. For instance, in the Yoga Sutras, it is believed that if you focus your attention on a place or an object, you will eventually be able to concentrate so fully that you will be able to blend into the object, or achieve union with it, and then you will be able to fully see the truth of that object.

Throughout the history of Western civilization, the literal, linear side has battled with the figurative, metaphorical side for predominance over the way we view life. And, as we know, ours is a culture in which the word has won over the image. For us, the intuitive, right-hemisphere type of thinking which perceives through symbols, feelings, images and poetry, has been subjugated to the rational, language-based processes.

However, there are some societies even today in which the reverse is true. In Bali, for instance, the spiritual world has more significance than the material world. There are cultures all over the world in which the lives of the people are related to their environment in emotional and physical ways, through ceremonies, dances, songs and drama. In these cultures, the people continually experience a connectedness with the universal, the mythical, the visible and the invisible realms.

In our culture, we have developed words which enable us to separate ourselves from our environment, until we have become unable to experience nature personally and internally. Rather, we stand back and analyze life for the purpose of manipulating it.

Earlier in history, language (heiroglyphs and ideographs, for example), corresponded to both universal and particuilar realities. These languages were based on images that were vivid parts of people's lives. Now we use words as tools to categorize experience so we don't have to respond to it.

However, it is still possible for us to to learn to see more accurately and to participate fully in the beauty of the world around us. We can do this by becoming aware of the details. When we become attentive to the world around us, we can become fully alive and in tune with all life and its potential for happiness and beauty.

The details all around us today are the essence of our existence. If we notice the fine points, we can appreciate this moment before it vanishes.

We can retrain ourselves to see the true images of the things around us instead of ignoring them. By noticing the beauty of nature all around, we live fully this moment, and we can develop a positive point of view as well.

Once we have become skilled observers, we can learn to use our inner vision to enrich our lives. This is the point at which mental development transcends words, and takes us past the immediate, literal and material world into the infinite.

When we use words to create a shallow layer of reality to justify our lower motives, our greed for power and control, our pettinesses, lusts, and jealousies, we can never really participate in the true beauty of existence, and we can never truly be alive. So we end up playing Monopoly instead of living.

This symbol reminds us that we can learn to utilize the powers of the beast and transform them into positive energy for life.

Chapter 10
The Hermit

The Hermit

The Hermit holds the lamp of truth. He represents the way-shower, illuminating the path for the seekers of the light. He is the source of all personal wisdom and the goal of every endeavor.

The Hermit

 **Y**ou have traveled far and you have seen much. You are walking in the dark, your path covered in shadows. You have taken the withdrawn and the introspective way in search of something that has been hidden.

The Hermit stands among the shadows. He has found inspiration, wisdom and peace of mind; he has found his soul.

He says to you:

I am _____

I see _____

I go _____

I have _____

I will _____

I must _____

I will follow _____

The secret message the Hermit tells you is:

_____

The Hermit has abandoned the conventions of society to follow his own inner convictions.

He is no longer merely a mirror reflecting the influences of outside circumstances.

The symbol of the Hermit represents prudence, caution and restraint, in favor of introspection.

The Hermit represents solitude and withdrawal into the self, where there is wisdom and peace.

Affirmation

Say to yourself:
I look inward, seeking the guidance of my higher self as I journey toward deeper understanding and
enlightenment.

This lovely ancient Mandean poem, quoted in Hans Jonas' <u>The Gnostic Religion</u>, expresses the symbolism of the Hermit, who looks within for a renewal of life and a conversion of the heart.

The Poem of the Hermit

From the day when we beheld thee,
from the day when we heard thy word, our hearts were filled with peace.
We believed in thee, Good One,
we beheld thy light and shall not forget thee.
All our days we shall not forget thee, not one hour let thee from our hearts,
For our hearts shall not grow blind,
these souls shall not be held back.

From the place of light have I gone forth, from thee, bright habitation...
An Uthra who accompanied me from the house of the Great Life
held a staff of living water in his hand.
The staff which he held in his hand
was full of leaves of excellent kind.
He offered me of its leaves,
and prayers and rituals sprang complete from it.
Again he offered me of them
and my sick heart found relief.
A third time he offered me of them,
and he turned upwards the eyes in my head
so that I beheld my Father and knew him.
I beheld my Father and knew him,
and I addressed three requests to him.
I asked him for mildness in which there is no rebellion.
I asked him for a strong heart
to bear both great and small.
I asked him for smooth paths
to ascend and behold the place of light.

From the day when I came to love the Life,
from the day when my heart came to love the Truth,
I no longer have trust in anything in the world.
In father and mother
I have no trust in the world.
In brothers and sisters
I have no trust in the world...
In what is made and created
I have no trust in the world.
In the whole world and its works
I have no trust in the world.
After my soul alone I go searching about,
which to me is worth generations and worlds.
I went and found my soul —
what are to me all the worlds?...
I went and found Truth
as she stands at the outer rim of the worlds... [8]

There are over 23 symbols in this illustration, including the "Truth, as she stands at the outer rim of the worlds..."

Looking at...

The Lamp

There is a lamp on the road before you. You pick it up. It shines upon the world, lighting everything in a new way.

You see _____

You realize _____

You understand _____

The lamp shows _____

It signifies _____

The lamp is your _____

Definition

The lamp represents the light of divinity, it is the symbol of immortality and wisdom. It also stands for guidance, especially divine guidance.

The things you see, realize and feel about the lamp are your own responses to wisdom and guidance. Your response to what the lamp is for you will indicate how you feel in terms of immortality and divine wisdom. Perhaps the lamp holds a message that can give you new insight and understanding.

Looking at...

The Cloak

Near the lamp you find a cloak. You put it on and you discover that it fits you perfectly. As the cloak envelopes you in its deep folds:

*You feel*_____

*You are*_____

*You can*_____

*You will*_____

*The cloak is your*_____

*Wearing this cloak you can*_____

Definition

The cloak is a symbol of withdrawl and obscurity. It can symbolize hiding and protection.

How do you feel about the cloak? Through this exercise you may discover the way you feel about withdrawing and hiding... it may seem threatening to you, and you may want to consider the advantages of having time and space for yourself away from the world. Or, the cloak may be welcome and feel safe. Do you withdraw a lot? Can you find reasons for your need to hide?

As with all of these exercises, you may find some insights into your own true nature in your responses to the questions.

The Staff

Resting against a tree, you find a staff. It is sturdy and you find that it fits your grip.

As you hold the staff in your hand, you realize _____

You feel _____

You understand _____

You have _____

The staff is your _____

With this staff you can _____

You put the staff _____

And you decide you will go _____

Definition

The staff represents masculine power, authority, dignity and magical power. It is also a symbol of a journey or a pilgrimage.

What can you learn about your inner feelings regarding power and dignity from your responses to the staff? Do you grasp it easily and eagerly? Or are you reluctant to take it?

What are your feelings about your journey or pilgrimage? Will you take up the staff and proceed? Or would you rather put it down and turn around?

Looking at...

The Cloak, the Staff and the Lamp

Now you are wearing the cloak. Your staff is in one hand and your lamp is in the other.

You feel _____

You can _____

You have _____

You will _____

You know _____

You see _____

Definition

The lamp, staff and cloak are the resources of the Hermit, who has withdrawn for inner guidance on his journey.

How do you feel about taking on the characteristics of the Hermit as you look inward for your own inner guidance along this pilgrimage to deeper personal understanding?

Do you have some negative responses? If so, can you find what has been blocking you?

Or are you eager and confident as you proceed along your journey? Do you have new insights to help you understand who you are and why you feel the way you do?

Taking Responsibility

e can always find answers to the problems that confront us in our lives, if we are willing to keep our minds open. First, however, we must operate on the assumption that there are answers to be found, which implies that there is some kind of meaning and coherence to life.

We are free to believe either that we are born for some purpose, or that we are insignificant. Because we have the choice of what to believe, clearly it is to our advantage to choose to believe in our own significance.

When we assume that life has meaning, our own lives become important; if we assume that something is true we will find the evidence which verifies that assumption.

We make choices every minute of our lives. Even when we are in a circumstance in which we seem to have no choice, we can choose how we will react to that circumstance.

However, usually we are in a position to make decisions and to take responsibility for the things that happen to us. We are in control of things. We control our actions and our reactions to people and experiences. Naturally, we do not have unlimited choices, but if we accept that fact and adjust our attitudes accordingly, we still remain in control of our reactions.

No matter how strong the forces may be, external conditions can not determine who and what we will become. We do that ourselves. We decide what we will do and it is we who must continually choose which way we will go.

Deciding on a Positive Perspective

When something goes wrong we could decide to see it as a sign of our ultimate failure and go no further. In that case, there is no doubt that unhappiness and displeasure would be forthcoming. On the other hand, we can use discouragement as a challenge to motivate us to fight harder, and we can decide to accept nothing less than our goal.

In order to live full lives we have to make positive choices for ourselves. Outside conditions are undeniably important, but we each have a say about who we are and who we will become. In addition, our attitude toward ourselves teaches others how to treat us.

If we can accept adversity as a natural part of life, we can find the energy to learn from it. When we no longer define hardship as our enemy, but accept it as a natural part of life, it can become a pivotal point in our development. We do not have to interpret adversity as an enemy, instead we can see it as an opportunity to grow.

Just deciding to make the assumption that we are significant and that life is meaningful is a way of taking responsibility for our lives. It prompts us to assess our experiences in an active way when we think of our lives in terms of what we can contribute. This activity itself is stimulating; this is the activity of life, and it brings with it its own satisfactions.

Pleasure and happiness are not passive experiences, and they are not found in retrospect. Usually we think of happiness as something that comes to us as we sit around waiting for it, but actually pleasure and happiness are active states. In fact, activity brings pleasure, and happiness comes from doing.

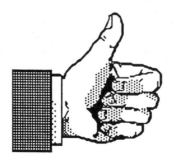